CLIFFHANGERS AND HILLSIDE HOUSES

Views from the Treetops

E. Ashley Rooney

Schiffer Publishing Ltd

4880 Lower Valley Road, Atglen, PA 19310 USA

Cover credits for the selected images-
Courtesy of Ron Ruscio Photography
Courtesy of J. Curtis Photography
2002 Erich Koyama
Spine- *Courtesy of Western Pennsylvania Conservancy*
Endpapers- *Courtesy of Moch. Sulthonn*
and Aji Mahareshi
Back cover- *Courtesy of Eric Figge Photography*

Library of Congress Cataloging-in-Publication Data

Rooney, E. Ashley.
    Cliffhangers and hillside houses : views from the treetops
/ E. Ashley Rooney.
        p. cm.
    ISBN 0-7643-2387-3 (hardcover)
    1. Architecture, Domestic—United States. 2. Hillside ar-
chitecture—United States. I. Title.

NA7208.R66 2006
728'.37—dc22
                                        2005037303

Cover and book designed by: Bruce Waters
Type set in Huminist 521/Helvetica

ISBN: 0-7643-2387-3
Printed in China

Published by Schiffer Publishing Ltd.
4880 Lower Valley Road
Atglen, PA 19310
Phone: (610) 593-1777; Fax: (610) 593-2002
E-mail: Info@schifferbooks.com

For the largest selection of fine reference books on this
and related subjects, please visit our web site at
www.schifferbooks.com
We are always looking for people to write books on new
and related subjects. If you have an idea for a book please
contact us at the above address.

This book may be purchased from the publisher.
Include $3.95 for shipping.
Please try your bookstore first.
You may write for a free catalog.

In Europe, Schiffer books are distributed by
Bushwood Books
6 Marksbury Ave.
Kew Gardens
Surrey TW9 4JF England
Phone: 44 (0) 20 8392-8585; Fax: 44 (0) 20 8392-9876
E-mail: info@bushwoodbooks.co.uk
Website: www.bushwoodbooks.co.uk
Free postage in the U.K., Europe; air mail at cost.

Acknowledgments

Tracking down cliffhangers is rather like embarking on a treasure hunt. There aren't many. You have to work hard. But when you find one, you marvel once again at the work of the architect who managed to design the residence so it could fit on that site and suit the client.

Over the Internet or through their work, I met many architects, who had fascinating approaches to their work and who have participated in helping to develop this collection of cliffhangers and hillside houses.

Joseph Henry Wythe, architect, played a major role in the creation of this book. As he says in his website, the United States has had an indigenous architecture for over one hundred years. In this book, we can see how the torch of creative imagination and sensitivity expressed by the great architectural pioneers — Louis Sullivan to Frank Lloyd Wright to Bruce Goff — has been passed on to the next generation of architects who adhere to the principles of organic architecture.

As I was completing the book, I met architect Jeremiah Eck. He reiterated the importance, the life-changing potential, of a thoughtfully designed home.

I must thank Clinton Piper of Western Pennsylvania Conservancy for his support; Kathy Shaffer for her insight; Richard Leo and Jane Fischer Johnson of Atlantic Archives Inc., who introduced me to Winterwood and Eric Schabacker and Joe Johnson; and Todos Santos Eco Adventures. Then there are the wonderful cameras of my husband, D. Peter Lund, and Paul Doherty and Robert Evans.

"Organic buildings are the strength and lightness of the spiders' spinning, buildings qualified by light, bred by native character to environment, married to the ground."
Frank Lloyd Wright

Frank Lloyd Wright's **Falling Water** has been acclaimed "the best all-time work of American architecture" and one of the "Top 50 Places of a Lifetime." *Courtesy of Western Pennsylvania Conservancy*

Contents

Foreword
Organic Architecture for Sloping Sites

Joseph Henry Wythe

The selection of a hillside for a dwelling site indicates that the special character of the place has touched souls. The dwelling to be designed for this unique site must meet the very special spiritual needs of not only those who will live there but all who will encounter it. When these deeper needs of the human soul have been fulfilled, it becomes a living architecture — organic.

Historically, few buildings other than those of Japan and the Gothic cathedrals of medieval Europe can qualify as organic architecture. Generally, the rooms were designed as rectangular boxes with rectangular holes punched into the walls for doors and windows. These sterile spaces were relieved by applied ornamentation to the surfaces, the generous amounts of furnishings stuffed into the rooms, and the liberal display of personal treasures wherever surfaces were available to place them. Dwellings for the affluent were ostentatious; all others, at best, were little more than shelter and only aspired to be showy. None were organic.

In the early twentieth century, Frank Lloyd Wright began a revaluation of the principles of domestic architecture resulting in the lovely dwellings that he designed for the prairies of the Midwest. This architecture he called "organic." As Wright's work expanded into other regions, he found those principles of organic architecture to be applicable to all types of buildings on all kinds of sites.

Eagle's Nest. A fantasy for a steep mountain canyon near Big Sur, California. Wythe visualized Eagle's Nest moving gently in the breeze, as a yacht rises and settles with the swells in the harbor. The U.S. State Dept. exhibited renderings of Eagle's Nest as an example of American architecture in embassies and US Information Agency offices around the world. *Courtesy of Joseph Henry Wythe*

This design is for a steep hillside with a spectacular view of San Francisco Bay. *Courtesy of Joseph Henry Wythe*

Moving from the upper terraces, down the steps into the recesses under the balconies, this house is the essence of organic architecture principles. *Courtesy of Joseph Henry Wythe*

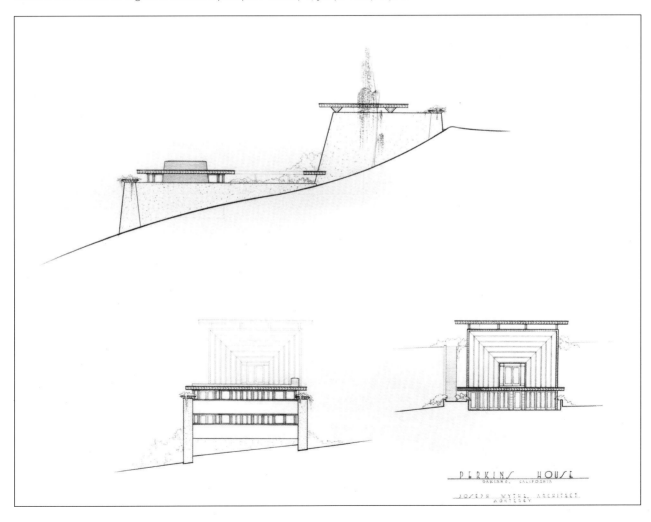

Among the first of these was Taliesin, the exquisite home that Wright built for his family and his apprentices on a Wisconsin hillside. His homes on the desert became integral parts of their surroundings. The beautiful dwellings he created for the slopes of Southern California and Lake Tahoe enhance the spirit of their places. Wright's masterpiece, Fallingwater, cantilevered over a creek in Pennsylvania, is universally recognized as one of the world's finest dwellings. In addition to the lovely dwellings he designed for the affluent, Wright was frequently challenged to create beautiful homes to be built on modest and even extremely limited budgets.

The many books now available showing the work of Frank Lloyd Wright may give an idea of what organic architecture is all about. However, only by actually moving through these spaces can one experience this architecture of delight. For those contemplating building a new home, visiting several buildings designed by Wright or others dedicated to the cause of organic architecture is recommended. Unfortunately, the number of these works is miniscule when compared to the vast amount of dismal construction we daily encounter, but these gems are well distributed throughout the country, so finding several whose owners are willing to show them should not be difficult.

Only in recent years have the architectural schools recognized the importance of the work of Frank Lloyd Wright. Since the faculties are still hardly aware of his principles of design, locating an architect dedicated to organic architecture may be something of a problem. However, the search will be worth the effort.

Now, let us investigate in greater detail what organic architecture is all about, particularly as it applies to dwellings on hillsides

Essence

On Building

Utility—A Building must serve well the various uses for which it is intended.

Economy—A Building must be constructed and maintained at a reasonable cost. The Building must retain its value with the passage of time.

Environment—A Building must be environmentally friendly, with consideration given to the use of materials that are renewable, using minimum amounts of total energy from the extraction, processing, shipping, and installation of the materials and in the operation and maintenance of the Building.

Reliability—A Building must be well built to resist the various deteriorating forces to which it could be subjected.

Comfort—A Building must be easy to use, with consideration given to proper lighting, climate control, sanitation, acoustics, circulation, and healthy environments.

On Architecture

Beauty—A Building becomes a Work of Architecture when it fulfills and transcends the requirements of practicality into the subjective realm of beauty.

Conception—A Work of Architecture is a true organism, inspired from the seed of an idea, nurtured with loving care, and brought into the full flowering of life.

Music—A Work of Architecture is a symphony of materials, composed to inspire the listener with passages ranging from simple harmonies to magnificent grandeur, from rest and repose to the exotic heights that stir the hearts of mankind.

Romance—A Work of Architecture is a delight, a joy to behold, to use, and to become a part of.

Integrity—A Work of Architecture proclaims a beauty of its own. It is free from the chains of past styles and current fads. The various materials used to express the beauty are inherent within. There is no sham or pretense.

Indigenous—A Work of Architecture is a part of the site, not merely a structure placed upon the site.

Nature—A Work of Architecture

is at one with Nature.

Time—A Work of Architecture, while an expression of its time in history, has a timeless quality that retains and enhances its beauty with the passing of years.

Mystery—A Work of Architecture has an aspect of mystery that intrigues the human mind to explore for new beauties inherent in the work.

Enhancement—A Work of Architecture enriches its community, the neighborhood, and the lives of those who encounter it.

Appeal—A Work of Architecture has universal appeal. Its enjoyment is not limited to a small band of esthetes and ascetics.

Creation—A Work of Architecture is an expression of the highest values of its culture, inspired by the creative imagination of the architect, and incorporating the dreams and aspirations of those who will use it. It demonstrates a faith in mankind to rise above all degrading and destructive forces.

Romance and the Organic

Amidst the clutter of this so-called civilization, there is occasionally a building that evokes a spiritual response, a feeling that imbues this work of architecture with the aspects of life and spirit — thus organic in nature. Its roots go deep into the natural world bringing forth profound emotions in those who encounter such places. Such a work of architecture is so much a part of its natural surroundings that it becomes at one with its site. The materials that have gone into the construction have been given life by the architect's imagination and sensitivity. Organic architecture is essentially romantic, even when using the most advanced technologies in the construction. This is truly a living architecture.

In discussing organic architecture, it is far more effective to describe those spiritual qualities of a static and inanimate structure as though the building really lives and moves as an organism. Some of these concepts date back to the dawn of history — a building "rising from the ground," or "thrusting skyward," or "vibrating with excitement." These are, of course, paradoxes; the building really does not rise, or thrust, or vibrate unless subjected to unusual dynamic forces. In a similar sense, we think of roofs hovering over walls, of spaces flowing around objects or interpenetrating with other spaces, of dynamic horizontal lines and planes, of components being in visual tension, of balance and repose. When the architect embraces these romantic concepts and uses technology only as a means to achieve the organic, then a great architecture will come into being.

Frank Lloyd Wright's 'Lieber Meister,' Louis Sullivan, begins his architectural ornament with a seed germ, which develops naturally into his wonderfully flowering of beauty. There is an exquisite order to this development, with each element of the design progressing naturally in harmony with that basic seed germ. If the seed germ is barren, the design will be without life, thus inorganic. But with life within that seed germ, the result will be a living architecture, a building with soul. This is "organic" architecture.

Reverence for Nature

A work of architecture can be created only through a reverence for the wonders of nature. Awe overcomes one beholding the multitude of natural forms including clouds, snow flakes, seasonal changes, birds and insects in flight, a leaf, caverns, flowers, sea shells, pine cones. Those who have lived in the mountains or forests feel touched by the biblical admonition, "I lift up mine eyes unto the hills from whence cometh my help."

Architecture and the Environment

Organic architecture is, by definition, a living architecture. The structure is at one and in harmony with its environment. It is shaped to protect itself from the various extremes of weather. It responds to the conditions of topography where it is located. It belongs to its site as the trees, rocks, and other features found there before any construction began. Indeed, a work of organic architecture can enhance the natural scene.

9

Frank Lloyd Wright lived most of his life in such an environment, excepting portions of his later years when he escaped to the desert in the winter. Those prairies were an integral part of his spiritual fiber, and he belonged to that land to the same extent as its grasses, shrubs, and wild life. The wide, open spaces of America's heartland were expressed in the strong horizontal lines of the roofs and belt courses in the prairie houses that Wright designed during the first two decades of the twentieth century. Buildings designed for the mountains, seashore, or urban environments will have different responses to their respective environments.

Idea and Order

Each work of architecture is based on an idea or combination of ideas that organizes the entire development of the design. It is the idea that gives the design its unity and strength. Lacking an idea, no project will ever become more than just another building; it will never achieve the life and spirit required for transcendence into a work of architecture.

The idea may be a structural concept, a geometric shape, powerful verticals, strong horizontals, heavy masses, delicate intricacies, the reflexive arrangement of the elements about an axis, or other organizing concepts including random or irregular lines and shapes. This basic idea may include additional ideas that are carefully inter-woven into the basic idea for contrast and counterpoint.

When each project is approached on its own terms, with an open mind, and not encumbered by reference to previous work, the idea can then blossom into a significant work of architecture. To be open to the possibility of being different prevents the mind from stagnating, from getting into a rut. Each problem encountered in the design is resolved as an individual solution specific to that design. By allowing full freedom for creative imagination, the designer becomes caught up in the excitement of exploration of new ideas. The result is a unique work of architecture, one designed specifically for its own set of unique requirements — individual — different from all others.

However, without the restraints of discipline, this freedom can degenerate into nothing more than license. Without discipline, an otherwise good idea becomes another cheap stunt that may attract attention but fails to become a work of architecture. The architect must instinctively know when to reject an idea that is inappropriate for the project. Is it in the order of "organization"? He must know when to stop. This discipline comes from experience and understanding the essence of the art. It provides the control to allow for the necessary order where all is in harmony.

Unfortunately, modern western society has no such structured order. The architect must be very specific about what is to go into the construction since there is no sense of order in any of the contractors, suppliers, or the workers in the trades. Even in the architectural offices, there can be only one designer who is in absolute charge of everything going on, unless other designers there are in complete understanding and harmony about the sense of order. That is why great architecture rarely comes from the efforts of a collaborative group and why the independent, interior decorator usually fails in achieving order.

Cohesion

Frank Lloyd Wright's "principle of pattern" seems to work marvelously well for many practitioners on architectural projects, although rarely as well as it worked for him. When a pattern coalesces, or presents itself, the solution to all of the problems encountered for that project will be found within that discovered pattern. It invariably produces the required solutions. This project pattern is uniquely appropriate for every design project and is derived from a particular site, the client, the program, an agreed upon budget, and, what is normally called the building climate. This "climate" is comprised primarily of the availability of materials, skills, and competent builders.

Bruce Goff, fully familiar with the thrill associated with finding appropriate solutions in this manner, explained this remarkable process as the concept itself. The concept assumes a life of its own and makes its inflexible demands upon the artist for all his time, knowledge, ability, and skill. Thus, the artist becomes slave to the concept with the absolute and imperative duty to bring the design to fruition and fully to its living form. It can be no surprise then that each of these creations, as in all natural growth or formation, bear the unmistakable DNA or stamp of its originator.

The Spirit Within

Bruce Goff told of being in an art dealer's shop one day when a soldier, recently returned from Japan, came in and unrolled an oriental scroll. "What's this"? the salty old proprietor demanded. "It's a painting of a tiger, and I paid a lot of money for it," the soldier nervously responded. "It's junk. Take it out of here. I don't want to see it," ordered the proprietor. "But, what's the matter with it"? inquired the disappointed seller.

"Well, just look at it. You see it all at once, don't you? A work of art, you never see it all at once."

It's hard to improve upon that crusty definition of works of art, including architecture. If a room can be seen almost all at once, it's not architecture. In organic architecture, one is continually discovering new delights — the relationships of lines, planes, and spaces; the changing light and shadows, patterns in the woodwork; the textures and other characteristics of the stonework. One never tires of it. One could spend a lifetime here and still marvel at new discoveries

Upon entering a building by Frank Lloyd Wright, one feels a sense of shelter, protection, and enclosure. There is a feeling of warm nurture here, particularly in dwellings where the heart of the home is the hearth. While the hearth may not be a cave, it is a place where one can feel secure, to read, to listen to music, to nap, or to just watch the flames dancing from the logs. Similar retreats can be created within the major living spaces. A nook or alcove away from the main activity

area can give the sense of cozy protection from extraneous distractions, where one can read or study without interruption.

Perhaps no room has a greater feeling of sterility than a pristine box with sleek furniture carefully placed just so, with the latest fads in paintings as selected by the decorator hung on the walls, and with no books in sight. Such a space may be exquisite to behold, but it is definitely not for human habitation. Aside from an elegant fashion model or mannequin, a person sitting in one of the chairs would appear to be out of place.

Adherence to the principles of organic architecture will provide the rich ambiance to the spaces within that will enhance the lives of all who encounter them.

Health and Well-being

"A building that is constructed from the heart will always evoke love in the people that come into contact with it. It makes people feel rejuvenated, positive, and at ease — a truly healing environment." David Pearson

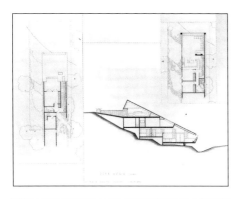

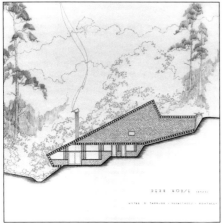

The site was a very narrow and steep lot with a small creek at the bottom. The clients loved to work in their garden and wanted the major rooms to open to the south. The roof, floors, and stairs cascade down, following the slope toward the creek. *Courtesy of Joseph Henry Wythe*

While careful attention to lighting, acoustics, air conditioning, and other technical items may be beneficial to the physical health of those who will use those buildings and, perhaps, to the economic health of those more interested in productivity and the bottom line, it is unfortunate that the equally important aspect of providing for the psychological and spiritual health of the occupants is almost completely neglected. A truly healthy building must go beyond the technical sciences that contribute to the physical health of the occupants, and must include the soul of the building that profoundly affects their spiritual health as well. Those buildings must give people a sense of self worth — that they and their activities are of value. They must heal, enrich, and create harmony within the community.

The resulting design follows the clients' desire for terraced gardens. The stairway and adjacent plant beds are illuminated by a strip sky-window. *Courtesy of Joseph Henry Wythe*

Houses are too often built without the spark of life that would make them homes of joy. Offices and other work places offer little incentive for meaningful production, as evidenced by the rush to leave when time is up. Schoolhouses fail to provide environments that help stimulate the minds of those forced to occupy their spaces. Commercial buildings scream for attention with their huge neon displays cluttering the streetscape, but offer no spiritual substance outside or within. Those buildings that are constructed expressly for healing offer little or nothing to help in the way of providing a nurturing environment.

In the inhuman buildings that have overwhelmingly blighted our environments, people tend to think and act in predominantly rational, coldly logical, and materialistic ways. People do respond to their surroundings. Why not provide conditions of delight?

This alternative design takes into account the clients' advancing years. Although gardening was limited to plant boxes on decks, the clients were fascinated with living among the birds. They selected this design. *Courtesy of Joseph Henry Wythe*

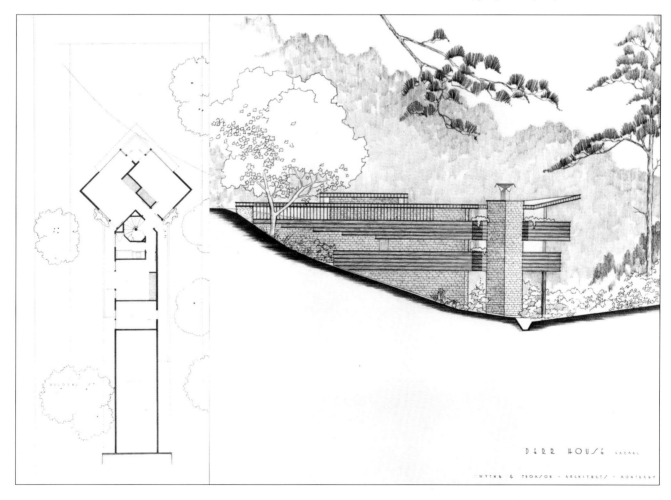

Organic Spaces

No work of art is more beautiful, more mysterious, more inspiring than that experienced in the modeling and flow of space in works of Nature. Fly through the woods with a song bird and delight in the ever changing vistas — swooping up into the tree canopies and the sky above, gliding among the massive tree trunks and limbs, darting back into the small spaces under the brush. Explore the three-dimensional world under the sea, moving around rocks and kelp, under and over ledges, back into caves and grottos.

This sense of mystery that comes with moving through sculptured spaces is one aspect of what Bruce Goff referred to as the continuous present. There is no beginning, no ending, only change. If there is no change, things become static — dead. Change is as vital to architecture as it is in nature. It is always present.

Even within the living room, you find the space flowing around other bends, up over overhanging ledges or into a balcony or mezzanine, back into an alcove and other cozy nook where you might retreat with a book. At the far end of the room, you see the space flow under a low soffit and around another bend, perhaps on into the dining space. You are led to explore further. This is a sense of movement, of always becoming,

To better understand this architecture of space, let us visit one of Frank Lloyd Wright's cre-

ations. From the entrance, a corridor stretches to the right leading to the living room, but you don't see that room; you only sense that it is there — around that bend at the far end of the corridor. Perhaps this is not really a corridor at all but a part of the living room since the partition, separating the two spaces is only about head height. The corridor ceiling is only a foot or so higher than the top of the partition and you see it extending out over a portion of the living room beyond. As you move along the corridor to the bend, you are aware of ever changing vistas and are intrigued to explore to find what is over the top of the partition. As you come around the bend, a

This house is sited on a steep hillside above Monterey Bay. The great room was the center of activities. As the children leave, bedroom partitions can be removed to expand the recreation area. *Courtesy of Joseph Henry Wythe*

ROSENBERG HOUSE
MONTEREY, CALIF.

JOSEPH WYTHE · ARCHITECT · MONTEREY

view of the living room begins to unfold, but not all at once. The low soffit above you extends a short distance into the living room. You become aware that the space that you are moving through is actually flowing around that bend, over the partition, and now — out from under the soffit on into the higher spaces of the room that you are just beginning to encounter.

Even within the living room, you find the space flowing around other bends, up over overhanging ledges or into a balcony or mezzanine, back into an alcove and other cozy nook where you might retreat with a book. At the far end of the room, you see the space flow under a low soffit and around another bend, perhaps on into the dining space. You are led to explore further. This is a sense of movement, of always becoming,

These living spaces are very much in evidence in the work of Frank Lloyd Wright and in the buildings of those who understand organic architecture.

This sculpturing of space, often called the interpenetration of space, is the alternative to the usual, sterile box kind of spaces — four walls, ceiling and floor — where the entrance is merely a hole cut into the wall and fitted with a door; where other holes called windows are cut into walls to let in light and to view the scene outside. Stepping through the doorway, you see the whole room all at once. In an organic space, the vistas come into view gradually as you move into the room; you never see it all in a glance.

Man is truly more than a two-dimensional creature. He responds positively to the mysteries of modeled spaces. He should not be denied.

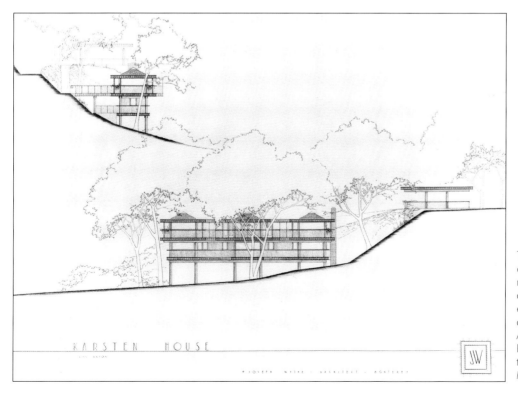

KARSTEN HOUSE

This house is sited under a high canopy of oaks on a steep north slope. Treated poles sunk deep into shale strata prevent earth movement and structural damage when the nearby San Andreas Fault goes into action. Pyramid roofs and skylights cap the poles. *Courtesy of Joseph Henry Wythe*

Architectural Honesty

No building can be a work of organic architecture if it is architecturally dishonest in any respect. Examples of such dishonesty abound, and the architect should always be alert to keep such dishonesty from creeping into his work.

In developing the dendriform columns for the Johnson Wax Building, Wright thought of those round columns in terms of Nature; the greatest resistance lateral forces is near its outer surface, and the inner core, not having much structural value, can be left hollow, as in a stalk of bamboo. His engineer, Mendel Glickman mentioned that "It would be easier and less expensive to construct the columns solid, and besides, nobody would know"; to which Wright solemnly responded, "Glick, you will know, and I will know, and God will know." End of argument.

Spirit of Place

Mental and physical health is seriously impaired in those who feel no spiritual connection with the places where they live, work, study, worship, and play. The human spirit must be in harmony with the spirit of place; otherwise, health and wellbeing suffer. Harmony with the spirit of the site renews the human spirit.

In the design of any project, whether it is a large tract or a small city lot, it is imperative that the architect considers all sites to be sacred places and takes ample time to make a number of pilgrimages to them — not only to determine their technical characteristics — but to get a feeling for their spiritual values. He must recognize that any development will change the spirit of place, perhaps to enhance it, perhaps destroy it completely. After such change, the spirit of place might be re-established, but usually, if at all, it will occur slowly, the time measured in human generations.

The spirit of place is essential for the needs of society in giving meaning, identity, purpose, and beauty to all who encounter the place. It enhances their well-being and even inspires the various arts. While understood by indigenous cultures, the concept of spirit of place is strange to most of our "civilized" society, resulting in the dismal conditions generally experienced in the developed world. The design professionals should lead this awakening.

Soul in Architecture

"I can think of no other time when it has been more important to consider the needs of the human soul. The twentieth century has been dominated by a worldview that glorifies a mechanistic, rationalistic focus at the expense of the inner life. The ravages that have been wreaked upon the planet as a result of this dissociation from the essential self have reached crisis proportions... Beyond the level of the rational mind is an awareness that without our souls, we are without our power, and without power, we will die." Marianne Moore, one of our most celebrated writers on spiritual subjects

An earth-sheltered building to be built on a narrow bench previously carved into the steep hillside. The greenhouse with hot tub is situated on a higher level behind the dwelling and illuminated by an A-frame skylight. *Courtesy of Joseph Henry Wythe*

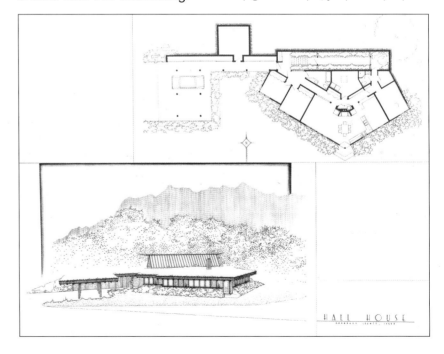

HALL HOUSE

While such terms as "spiritual," "soul," and "sacred" may have a religious significance to many, they are used here to describe feelings, experiences, and meaning to life that are deeper and more profound than the intellectual level. From the soul flows a sense of sacredness, enrichment, inspiration, and meaning to life. We are related and connected to an "other" that is greater than oneself, but not necessarily a supernatural being. Such terms express an intuitive form of experience capable of evoking various emotional responses.

"...A genuine appreciation of beauty can only result in silence... When you behold the daily wonder of the sunset, have you ever thought of applauding?" Claude Debussy

As in music, the same spirit touches our souls upon encountering beauty in nature and works of architecture and the other arts. In many ways, architecture is frozen music, and the drama of moving through its spaces and recesses gives feelings and responses similar to being carried along with the flow of a musical composition. The religious experience of a Gothic cathedral is as much a feeling of wonder as of devotion to the divine. We respond naturally, not merely from a sense of duty, which, unfortunately, is required in the dead spaces now designed for worship.

However, being in the presence of beauty can bring forth a variety of spontaneous emotions and responses ranging from a gentle softness and reverent silence to shouts of joy, delight, rapture, ecstasy, love, song, dance, and expressions of power. Our spirit is inspired by the living nature of the environment in which we find ourselves. A sensitive architect will design live spaces for the various purposes so that our deepest feelings will naturally respond in harmony and our souls will be touched.

Situated on a steep hillside, this house has a bedroom designed for watching the moon rise over the mountains across the lake. *Courtesy of Joseph Henry Wythe*

This passive solar, earth-sheltered house is on a steep slope. *Courtesy of Joseph Henry Wythe*

Such soul responses are not confined to religious buildings or even dwellings. Indeed, the psyche responds positively to living architecture in classrooms, offices, factories, stores, hotels, theaters, and the countless other places of human activities, including our towns and cities. We feel and function well in spaces that are designed to be spiritually alive, where the spaces are in natural and complete harmony with the souls of those who will encounter the spaces.

Each building material has spiritual qualities of its own that will affect the soul of the place. We tend to respond to materials in their natural state or which have received minimal processing, thus revealing their natural colors, patterns, and textures. High-tech products, on the other hand, may inspire with their highly imaginative innovations, but they are often spiritually dead.

We are attuned to the inner reality of the spaces, where we instinctively understand what the place says to us. We "know" if we belong there or should back off. Does the space make us feel good or ill? A visitor to one home commented that when she came in she immediately felt that, "The house liked her, that it felt like the house was putting its arms around her and welcoming her." We are capable of picking up the most subtle nuances of the ambiance of spaces. If anything offends, we are aware of it, even though we may not be able to identify what it is.

When all of these sensual aspects of a building are in harmony, it becomes a work of architecture; it has soul, which nourishes and heals the human spirit. These places feel alive, and we respond with delight. Furthermore, studies have indicated that the feelings that are stimulated by such places with soul are indeed healthy, both physiologically and psychologically. Architecture with soul conveys a sense of love coming from unconditional giving, a rich, rewarding, enduring, and respectful relationship with the people whom it touches.

True architecture is life enhancing. To touch the souls of the people, it must have a soul of its own. No place of work, or study, or worship, or play, or any other human activity should be depressing in spirit. Our built environment must be in harmony with nature and the human essence; it must be uplifting to the entire community. The architecture of delight creates the necessary conditions for the joy of living. It is a tremendous responsibility for all design professionals to thoroughly understand the human psyche, to have a keen appreciation of beauty of all kinds, and to create works of architecture that will enhance the environment and all forms of life within.

Joseph Henry Wythe became a journeyman carpenter before studying architecture. At the University of Oklahoma, he studied under his mentor, Bruce Goff. Although not an apprentice to Frank Lloyd Wright, Wythe often visited Mr. Wright at Taliesin and elsewhere. For several years following graduation in 1948, Wythe remained at OU to teach design and several technical courses. Returning to California, Wythe opened his studio in Monterey. At the local community college, he taught an innovative beginning course in architecture, which became so successful that students transferring to the University reported receiving two years of credit for the one-year course at Monterey. In 1977, Wythe moved to Sandpoint, Idaho, where he established his studio under the name of Alternative Architecture and later constructed his home and studio, Unicorn Farm.

Wythe is author of the books *Drawings for an Alternative Architecture; Flights of Fancy,* and *Prelude to Design.* The above article is an excerpt from the manuscript of his next book, *Alternative Architecture: Essence and Education.* Descriptions of these books and additional writings and illustrations are shown on the web site, www.alternative-architect.com

1. Introduction

Throughout history, people have wanted to live at the top of the hill. Medieval knights could see who was coming, the rich landowner could look down on his crops, and the society matron could enjoy her stunning view of the sea or the mountains. For a great many of us, the notion of living on a hill conjures up images of a castle in the Alps, a cabin in the Adirondacks, or a house overhanging the roar of the Pacific. We want to be at the top of the hill – or at least among the treetops — having made it this far in our lives. Living at the top is a great place to be and an attractive status symbol.

Many towns have "hills" where the more luxurious houses are found. In our town of approximately 30,000 inhabitants, we have three hills. All three are the sites of some of the best homes in town: the ones that sell at overwhelming prices and whose owners have the instincts, the checkbook, and the stamina to renovate and maintain them to their best style. In the past, large residences with garages, barns, or gatehouses occupied vast areas on these hills, but today the lots are divided and subdivided as suburbia continues its sprawl. Now, many more houses than there were 50 years ago are situated on these hills.

In many areas of the United States, houses are stacked up on hillsides – each elbowing the next in order to grab some of the view. They sit side-by-side on the arid hillsides. They tower over the highways. Some residences might even be considered expensive non entitities in their lack of design integrity, environmental sustainability, human safety, and wellbeing.

Views from the treetops: a spring storm over Beaver Lake. *Courtesy of Eric T. Schabacker*

Some watch TV at dinner; others marvel at the beauty of the land. *Courtesy of Richard Leo Johnson/Atlantic Archives.com*

A Pacific sunset. *Courtesy of Robert D. Evans*

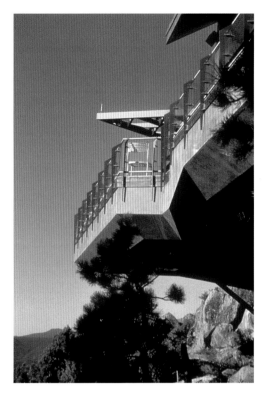

A view of a cantilevered deck from below. ©Ronforth/Ronforthphoto.com

California cliff crowded with residences.
Courtesy of Eric Figge Photography

A slope in Utah. *Courtesy of Paul Doherty*

A cliffhanger on a Massachusetts highway. *Courtesy of D. Peter Lund*

In other areas, these residences are beautiful, distinctive, and affordable. They look over flower-strewn meadows, track the stars over the towering snow-capped mountains, or revel in the vibrant nightlights of the bustling city. Well sited, they fit with their site, complementing their environment. They are houses with soul!

In some cases, they are at the foot of the hill. Those houses get to look up to the stars. In others, they are in the trees on the side of the hill.

In short, the hill is a great place to live – whether you are at the top, somewhere in the middle, or at the bottom. But to live well on a hill, you need a thoughtfully designed home that is integrated into the site.

Finding an ideal location for a cliffhanger or hillside home is a major challenge. In many densely settled areas, desirable land for building is hard to come by. Setback requirements, property lines, runoff, septic systems, and other factors are just some of the few legally defined setbacks. Then there are the sightlines identified to preserve the neighbors' views, the need to preserve tree roots, concerns about climate and weather, and the desire for sun and panoramic views.

Both environmental factors and governmental restrictions have increased the difficulties involved in finding available property. As one Vermonter pointed out, when people build on the ridgeline they may destroy others' view of that hill. Nevertheless, navigating local building codes and zoning ordinances can be done. The question is whether it can be done with taste and appropriateness.

Ideally, a house should be so much a part of its natural surroundings that it becomes at one with its site. Frank Lloyd Wright, America's premier architect, once commented: "No house should ever be on the hill or on anything. It should be of the hill, belonging to it. Hill and house should live together."

The United States certainly has many beautiful hilltop sites. They range from our majestic mountains to rolling hills to rocky cliffs overlooking the ocean. It is up to you and your architect whether your home will become part of the hill or a glaring eyesore.

A cliffhanger on the rocky coast of Maine. *Courtesy of D. Peter Lund*

A cliffhanger in New England. *Courtesy of D. Peter Lund*

This single-family residence designed by RKD Architects is situated on a steep and dramatic site in the Rocky Mountains. *Courtesy of Ron Ruscio Photography*

Hidden in the forest within the Ozark Mountains of northwest Arkansas, just outside of Eureka Springs, sprawls Winterwood, an eighty-five acre lakeside estate. *Courtesy of Eric T. Schabacker*

This Italian style villa designed by Debra Kay George Interiors is perched on the edge of a hill in Los Gatos, California. *Courtesy of Ken Huenin.*

2.
Top of the Hill

Many of us have dreamed about living among the clouds high above the treetops. Perhaps we want to escape the world; perhaps we want to soar with the birds. Living on a hill can be something special.

Houses on the hills can make a major statement. We notice their placement, their size, perhaps a unique feature. To paraphrase John Winthrop, "for when we must consider that when we are a house upon a hill, the eyes of all people are upon us."

Connecticut River Overlook

Living on the Connecticut River is beautiful: from the first tender green days of spring when pastel blooms paint the hills to those warm June days when boats of all sizes and types fill the river to the cool crisp days of fall when the countryside blazes red, gold, and orange.

When winter comes and snowflakes fall into the murmuring water, life on the water changes. People leave, and the land becomes quiet again with only the snapping, crackling ice punctuating the cold. New animals appear, and the chimney smoke settles into the valleys.

Jonathan Isleib of JBI Design knows this country well. He designed this house so his clients could be a part of that land.

A close-up of the library corner of house shows the exposed ledge and transplanted native moss from the property. The custom charcoal gray stucco walls allow the body of the house to dramatically recede into nature's trees and rocks. *Courtesy of James T. Abts, Hamilton, Massachusetts*

Details are an important touch. The Japanese lantern on the stone pier is part of the fieldstone enclosure to the auto court. Native blueberry bushes on the hillside were protected during construction. Entrance to the foyer and carp pool is between the two gigantic boulders at the center of the photo. *Courtesy of James T. Abts, Hamilton, Massachusetts*

The octagonal, river view room is on the left with terrace at top under the charcoal gray stucco chimneys. Terraced stonewalls allow access around the house and the structure to blend into the rocky hillside. *Courtesy of James T. Abts, Hamilton, Massachusetts*

The foyer, which leads to bridge across the pool to the auto court, has Jerusalem gold limestone floor with bluestone border, maple trim, and Japanese chests. The circular window highlights the cove past the terrace. *Courtesy of James T. Abts, Hamilton, Massachusetts*

Dining area overlooks carp pool entrance and ledge hillside. The table's 5-foot square shape was the inspiration for the 90-degree over scale bay window/dormer. The red cedar ceiling adds warmth. *Courtesy of James T. Abts, Hamilton, Massachusetts*

Great room has orange leather sofa and Tibetan rug of traditional design. The ceiling is red cedar; the floors are curly maple random-width. Foyer is beyond the center. *Courtesy of James T. Abts, Hamilton, Massachusetts*

The dining bay is adjacent beyond the mudroom door and garages; the bridge crosses the carp pool to foyer entrance. The field stone band integrates house into the ledge surroundings. *Courtesy of James T. Abts, Hamilton, Massachusetts*

The home office has the deck beyond and breathtaking view of the water below. *Courtesy of James T. Abts, Hamilton, Massachusetts*

Breakfast/luncheon skylight bay overlooks the tidal cove and floating deck beyond the kitchen to left. Jonathan Isleib, the architect, designed the custom corner sofa. *Courtesy of James T. Abts, Hamilton, Massachusetts*

A bluestone terrace surrounds the octagonal sunroom. It has a limestone floor and bluestone border, Atlantic white cedar ceiling, and a panoramic view of the cove. *Courtesy of James T. Abts, Hamilton, Massachusetts*

Master bathroom affords dramatic views to the water and rocky hill into which the house was integrated. The shower is seen in the mirror with a pair of windows above a built-in seat. There are 2-inch thick teak counters at the dual sinks; limestone floors, white cedar walls, and curly maple wall. *Courtesy of James T. Abts, Hamilton, Massachusetts*

The master bedroom has a Japanese altar table and screen to left and custom 5 1/2-inch louver blade shutters. There is maple trim at ceiling, base, and floorboard. The view is of the cove beyond. *Courtesy of James T. Abts, Hamilton, Massachusetts*

Guest room overlooks intermediate terrace garden with main terrace above to the right. The corner window with its view of the cove is typical of the architect. *Courtesy of James T. Abts, Hamilton, Massachusetts*

The guest bath also plays to the importance of the views. Caramel-colored Travertine tile blends with the teak counter and maple trim. *Courtesy of James T. Abts, Hamilton, Massachusetts*

The custom monorail stair to the lower level has 3-inch maple treads. The large floor-to-ceiling windows at top of stairs flood the lower level with afternoon western light; maple flooring is random width; Japanese chest is to the right. *Courtesy of James T. Abts, Hamilton, Massachusetts*

The long silhouette of terraces and the grey-colored stucco, which help the house appear to be at ease with its surroundings, do not detract from the dramatic impact of the octagonal room. *Courtesy of James T. Abts, Hamilton, Massachusetts*

This photo shows how the house embraces the ledge hillside. *Courtesy of James T. Abts, Hamilton, Massachusetts*

Laguna Beach Italian Villa

The clients requested that Brion Jeannette create a home on the cliffs of Laguna Beach, California, that would allow them to feel like they were living on their much-loved Italian coast. Brion Jeannette not only met the client's goals but also his own professional goal of maximizing natural light and ventilation while blending energy-efficient design technology and green strategies.

Unassuming from the street, Brion Jeanette's design appears to be a collage of texture and intrigue. Behind the entry gate, you are welcomed into unending surprises. *Courtesy of Eric Figge Photography*

This casual but elegant Italian villa hugs the cliff, creating level changes throughout the home, reminiscent of the old world villas that evolved through many different generations. Decks and patios at every level embrace the breathtaking ocean views of southern California and allow for intimate dining on the rooftop or a playful swim in the lower grotto. *Courtesy of Eric Figge Photography*

Once inside the street entry gate, you are overcome by beautiful views. *Courtesy of Eric Figge Photography*

The entry courtyard brings a warm welcome.
Courtesy of Eric Figge Photography

The entire villa opens to the outside. Expansive sliding doors recede, permitting gracious living both inside and out. *Courtesy of Eric Figge Photography*

Living room and outside patios invisibly blend one to the other. *Courtesy of Eric Figge Photography*

This house is designed for entertainment. Glass prisms in the ceiling cast a soft glow of alternating color as the sun travels over the villa throughout the day. *Courtesy of Eric Figge Photography*

Preparing and sharing meals are the "real" entertainment center of this villa. The dining patio also has a brick pizza oven. *Courtesy of Eric Figge Photography*

The master suite enjoys ocean views and spacious intimacy. *Courtesy of Eric Figge Photography*

Several private suites are available for guests. Each is unique as the villa itself – why would you ever want to leave? *Courtesy of Eric Figge Photography*

Hand formed concrete with an old world finish keeps the wine cellar at the perfect temperature. Select the right Chianti or Barolo for afternoon refreshment; what a recipe for an easy afternoon of shared stories! *Courtesy of Eric Figge Photography*

You can dine on the roof garden overlooking the Pacific Ocean. *Courtesy of Eric Figge Photography*

Sewanee Retreat

Twenty-three state parks, covering some 132,000 acres as well as parts of the Great Smoky Mountains National Park, Cherokee National Forest, and Cumberland Gap National Historical Park are in Tennessee. This fertile bluegrass state is known for its beautiful, lush green scenery.

The clients wanted a home that would function as a family retreat for weekend getaways as well as summer and holiday gatherings. Maurice Jennings + David McKee Architects created a dynamic 3,900 square foot family vacation home sited at the edge of a bluff overlooking a forested valley.

A bridge connects the auto court to the main entry below a single low-slope gable roof. The north wall of the residence is generally unglazed and screens views to the auto court while focusing views through the southern glazing. On the south side of the building, generously glazed walls overlook the bluff and bring the outdoors into the building. The loft level overlooks the grand main space that focuses views to the south. The lower level contains private areas such as bedrooms and bathrooms.

The sloping site allowed clustering four bedrooms on the lower level while opening up to the bluff edge to the south. Cypress siding protected by a standing seam copper roof along with native stone columns, walls, and a large central stone fireplace, work together to unite the structure with the site.

A footbridge connects the parking area to the main entry. The nearly solid entry facade withholds the dramatic view to the valley. *Courtesy of Richard Leo Johnson/ Atlantic Archives.com*

From the west elevation of the residence, you can see both the bridge that connects the auto court to the main entry and the cantilevered balcony. *Courtesy of Richard Leo Johnson/Atlantic Archives.com*

This view is from the bluff side balcony looking towards the house. The entry is below a single low-slope gable roof. *Courtesy of Richard Leo Johnson/ Atlantic Archives.com*

In this view from the balcony looking north-west, you can see how the roofing reflects the stepping of the house plan. This stepping allows for panoramic views from the master bedroom. *Courtesy of Richard Leo Johnson/ Atlantic Archives.com*

The balcony of this contemporary vacation home juts out over the Cumberland Plateau, the largest remaining forested plateau in the continental United States. The house is sited so that it appears to have emerged directly from the bluff. *Courtesy of Richard Leo Johnson/Atlantic Archives.com*

View from the lower level looking southeast. The native stone site walls help tie the structure to the bluff edge. *Courtesy of Richard Leo Johnson/ Atlantic Archives.com*

The main level is kept open and airy as the living, dining, and kitchen functions share a common space. Looking west from the dining area, the ridge skylights provide natural illumination deep into the house. *Courtesy of Richard Leo Johnson/ Atlantic Archives.com*

Looking east from the living area, the open plan allows gathering spaces to be visually connected. *Courtesy of Richard Leo Johnson/Atlantic Archives.com*

In this view, we are looking over the southern vista framed by the window mullions. The geometric pattern established in the glass subdivision repeats throughout the home in screen door stiffeners and custom wood light fixtures. *Courtesy of Richard Leo Johnson/Atlantic Archives.com*

View looking southeast over kitchen counter. The butt-jointed glass corners visually dissolve the boundary between inside and outside. *Courtesy of Richard Leo Johnson/Atlantic Archives.com*

Adjacent to this multi-function living area is the master bedroom and dressing area. Mullions echo the form of the roof and frame the view to the adjacent forest. *Courtesy of Richard Leo Johnson/Atlantic Archives.com*

A loft space, which serves as both home office and extra sleeping space, overlooks the great room. *Courtesy of Richard Leo Johnson/Atlantic Archives.com*

The overlook allows the loft space to borrow spatially from the living area below. It is a great area for working and dreaming. *Courtesy of Richard Leo Johnson/Atlantic Archives.com*

The balcony extends the living space, providing the family with an area for dramatic views and outdoor gathering. *Courtesy of Richard Leo Johnson/Atlantic Archives.com*

Come Fly with Me

To capitalize on the view, architect Robert Oshatz designed a 4,000 square foot home, which rises above trees and utility lines to a spectacular view of the valley. The back of the house is anchored into the hillside opening out to a courtyard. From this anchor, the living room floats out into space cantilevering 28 feet, giving you the feeling of floating in space — instead of looking out at the view; you feel you are part of the view!

From the street-level garage, you can take an elevator to all levels of the house. The entry courtyard stairs lead to a roof top garden above the garage, where you can either continue up by stair or elevator. The third level above the street contains the formal entry to the house, two bedrooms with private baths, and a recreation room. The fourth level contains the living room, dining room with access to a courtyard and swimming pool beyond, the kitchen, and master bedroom suite.

From the living room, the exterior fins shield the view of the utility poles and lines. *Courtesy of Michael Arden*

The numerous windows and skylights add to the light and airy feeling. *Courtesy of Michael Arden*

From the outer edge of the living room, you can glimpse other parts of the house. Behind the mirror-faced fireplace is the elevator that opens out a few stair steps above the dining room. *Courtesy of Michael Arden*

The kitchen has a built-in breakfast area and window seat. The circular window with its valley view is composed of 12-inch strips of glass cemented together with silicone. *Courtesy of Michael Arden*

The kitchen sink counter faces a large window looking into the courtyard. *Courtesy of Robert Oshatz*

The circular hole in the wall connects the kitchen to the bar alcove and living room beyond. *Courtesy of Robert Oshatz*

California Mediterranean

When the clients decided to build their home above Laguna Beach's coastal cliffs, they sought the creative talent of architect Brion Jeannette. Together, they created a stately, home that permits hospitable entertaining and accommodates the couple's family and friends for extended visits. Brion Jeannette designed several guest suites within an easily closed off wing of the home. The separate pool house also doubles as a guest suite.

Perched on a steep cliff above the Pacific Ocean, this 11,000 square foot contemporary Mediterranean home has a stately grace. *Courtesy of Eric Figge Photography*

This home has an abundance of natural light and ventilation. *Courtesy of Eric Figge Photography*

The formal driveway approach announces the fact that this home is important yet inviting. Existing native pines were preserved to enhance this cliff top home. *Courtesy of John Connell Photography*

The entry is designed to let the visitor know the people who live here have tremendous respect for tradition but embrace a more modern lifestyle. *Courtesy of John Connell Photography*

The entry foyer is the central welcoming axis. The stair to the right leads to the guest wing; directly ahead is the private library/office. The formal living room is to the left. *Courtesy of Eric Figge Photography*

The richly paneled library and home office creates an appropriate environment for business affairs and provides a comfortable space for planning fun adventures. The spiral stair leads to an extensive library and additional guest suite. *Courtesy of Eric Figge Photography*

The great room is the center of daily life. The spacious kitchen with multiple ovens, warming drawers, and other appliances allows for endless culinary experiences. A generous butler's pantry (on the right) permits final food prep before serving a meal in the formal dining room. *Courtesy of Eric Figge Photography*

Architect Brion Jeannette encircled the breakfast area in glass to capitalize on the spectacular views. *Courtesy of Eric Figge Photography*

This house was born to party. The
dramatic landscaped site is enjoyed both
from the formal living room on the left and
the intimate family center of the great
room on the right. The large outdoor
barbecue with bar seating allows guests to
keep a watchful eye on the cook.
Courtesy of Eric Figge Photography

Multiple layers of architectural detailing on
the eaves add a dimension of strength and
stateliness to the design. *Courtesy of John
Connell Photography*

Waterfront Site

Siting a house on the water may seem easy, but it's not always so simple. You have to integrate the structure with the land and the natural features. Then there is the climate and the need for enclosure, protection, and durability. Most sites on the water also have many wetland regulations associated with them. Depending on the house's proximity to the water, these regulations can have a major impact on the design of the house, affecting not just the site but also the view.

The problem that faced Jeremiah Eck Architects was that the house had to be built behind a parallel line 100 feet back from the water's edge. Additional zoning requirements required setbacks from the street, resulting in a long and narrow footprint. Consequently, only one side of the house would capture the spectacular views of the Atlantic.

The firm saw this as an opportunity, however. The living room, kitchen, and master bedroom all have great views. The other rooms have less, and the entry has no view at all. In fact, when you enter the house you're not even aware of the view. By keeping the entry away from the view, the rest of the house takes full advantage of it.

Another challenge was the rocky Atlantic coastline. Rather than removing it, the firm decided to have the floor step down from the entry to the living levels over the rocky slope towards the water. The study, living/dining room, and decks are just two steps up from the rocks. The result: a house that fits naturally on its site.

The regulatory setbacks from the water's edge and the street determined the rectangular plan of the house, parallel to the water's edge. *Photo by Anton Grassl*

The exterior deck steps down gradually over the length of the house, responding to the topographic changes and culminating in a useful ledge to sit on. *Photo by Anton Grassl*

A primary advantage of placing the house parallel to the water is that many rooms have a dramatic view of the rocky coastline. *Photo by Anton Grassl*

The angular shapes of the roofs reflect and blend with the jagged quality of the rocky shoreline below. *Photo by Anton Grassl*

A good floor plan can convey what is important in our lives. *Photo by Anton Grassl*

For some it may be the hearth. *Photo by Anton Grassl*

Whether the property is a rocky outcrop over the ocean or a small site on a gentle hill, the goal in siting a house is to integrate the structure with the natural features surrounding it. *Photo by Anton Grassl*

Sometimes siting a house is straightforward; other times it takes some creativity to achieve the union of a house with its site, the man-made and the natural. *Photo by Anton Grassl*

Michigan Cliffside Retreat

Designed by Moiseev/Gordon Associates, Inc., this estate-sized Frank Lloyd Wright-inspired home was a challenge to locate on the steeply sloping, wedge-shaped, lakefront lot. The site organization resulted in a dramatic stepped and setback elevation, which enlivens the facade, softens the masses of the home, and captures generous, multi-faceted views to the lake from virtually every room.

The traversing drive arrives at a limestone entry and the rough-hewn brick and wood exterior. Stepping through the leaded glass door into a traditional vestibule immediately sets the tone for the blending of old world elegance with the modern conveniences of today. The home is equipped with many generous and free flowing rooms designed exclusively for gracious entertaining.

The skillfully selected interior furnishings blend the best of French style with understated overtones of art deco. Streamlined furniture defines multiple groupings for intimate gatherings beneath a period chandelier acquired from the demolished department store, Hudson's, once located in downtown Detroit. The interior designers were Richard Ross of Richard Ross Designs and Jeffrey King of Jeffrey King Interiors.

White-glove parties and blue-jean weekends can both feel at home in the elegant yet comfortable setting. An elevator can whisk you from floor to floor once the end of the day arrives. Whether enjoying hors d'oeuvres atop the intimate wood beamed loft, enjoying a cool breeze in the screen-in porch, or taking in a movie from the plush upholstered chairs in the media room, you experience an all encompassing luxury known only to the few.

The two-story great room's grand bay window offers sweeping views of the lake from its high perch on the bluff. *Courtesy of Vaughn Gurganian*

The facade is enlivened with a multi-stepped roof and a faceted facade, maximizing lake views. *Courtesy of Vaughn Gurganian*

This aerial view shows how the home sits high in the trees looking down on to the lake far below. *Courtesy of Vaughn Gurganian*

The driveway curves towards the main door of the French inspired stone and brick exterior. *Courtesy of Vaughn Gurganian*

Beautiful brickwork and stone detailing sets the tone for this estate above the lake. *Courtesy of Vaughn Gurganian*

The beautifully beamed and coffered ceiling sweeps from the balcony above, across the great room to the window wall beyond. *Courtesy of Vaughn Gurganian*

The view from the balcony reveals the lake below as well as the antique chandelier. *Courtesy of Vaughn Gurganian*

The tray ceiling and beautiful details of the dining room enrich the experience of an intimate dinner party. *Courtesy of Vaughn Gurganian*

The elegant master bedroom maximizes the sweeping vaulted view of the lake below. *Courtesy of Vaughn Gurganian*

The functional modern kitchen is beautified with custom cabinetry and an antique "side board." It has easy access to a walk-in pantry, office area, elaborate butler's pantry, and elevator. *Courtesy of Vaughn Gurganian*

The Cliff House

Perched on a 120-foot-tall granite ridge at 9,000 feet above sea level, this residence designed by Sears Barrett spins glass corners into sweeping views of the Rockies. The sensation is similar to flight with distant peaks in all directions and an emerald green lake below.

The site is an angular, rugged spine of stone that provides an edge beyond which there is only the lake far below. There are few trees and little room to move as the property line parallels the ridge just 50 feet away.

Through rotating three interlocking forms, the plan generates a series of glass corners that project out over the rocks to frame the view. A large central living room and the adjacent kitchen give a spatial center to the plan. The master suite and study are above and to one side, while the guest bedrooms and sitting room are below and to the other side. At the entry, an outer layer comprised of columns provides a linking framework that joins the separate pyramidal roofs. A tree grows through the entry frame as one ascends to the doorway.

The pyramidal roofs read as strong and simple forms in this powerful setting. The corners of the structure turn to meet the geometry of the site and provide the eye an opportunity to sweep across the horizon. Decks cantilever beyond the edge of the cliff at one point and then return to vertical rock mass for support. This is a place where the earth moved upward with massive geological force. Balanced carefully on the edge, the cliff house is capped with a symbolic set of peaks clad in the color of the forest.

This mountain home is perched on a cliff 200 feet above a lake in the Colorado Rockies. A massive rock formation erupts from the cliff edge directly in front of the living room window. *Courtesy of J. Curtis Photography*

A pair of rotated hip roofs is all that can be seen of the house above the forest. Snow-capped peaks surround the house in every direction. *Courtesy of J. Curtis Photography*

Deep overhangs shelter the glass from the intense sunlight at the 9,000-foot elevation. The entry wall is set in a frame that is pulled forward from the building mass. *Courtesy of J. Curtis Photography*

This frame acts like a front porch sheltering the front door and framing the stairway glass. The center portion of the porch, however, has no roof in order to provide sunlight to a planter below. *Courtesy of J. Curtis Photography*

The plan is based on three rotated squares, which provide dramatic corners of glass projecting into the view. In this view, the lake is visible below and Breckenridge Mountain is in the distance. *Courtesy of J. Curtis Photography*

A detail view of the fireplace and television cabinet in the living room. Minimal trim detailing with cabinets and fireplace surround slightly recessed into the plane of the wall lends a crisp uncluttered feel. Simplicity in detailing and trim lets the eye focus on the magnificent view beyond. *Courtesy of J. Curtis Photography*

A winter view of the glass corner in the living room. Snow covers the rock formation, which sits just beyond the corner window. A deck to the left of the rock is accessible through sliding glass doors. *Courtesy of J. Curtis Photography*

The kitchen opens to an informal hearth room, which allows for seating around a fireplace or casual meals. The sunlit deck and flawless views beyond open the room to winter landscapes. *Courtesy of J. Curtis Photography*

The kitchen is located at the center of the plan. The living room fireplace can be seen framed in the opening, which serves as a bar and buffet. A sliding panel in the overhead cabinet provides the option of separating the two rooms visually. *Courtesy of J. Curtis Photography*

The Forgotten Lot

Just blocks from Boise's historic East End neighborhood, a forgotten lot in a 1970s subdivision sat for over 30 years, unworkable to most. Its dramatically steep slope prohibited the typical site preparation of flattening the land. The goal for Trout Architects was to construct an affordable residence with a separate, adjacent artist studio/apartment that fully exploited the city and desert views as well as the intimacy offered by the narrow foothills site.

The two counter-opposing structures are notched deep into the site. Above the main house located higher up on the hill, the separate artist studio south of the entry stairs offers privacy, additional entertaining space, a deck, and a full bathroom.

Warm and inviting, this home serves as both form and function for creativity. Here, we see the view up from the southeast entry. Large windows open on to views of the sky and the land.
© 2004 Deborah Hardee

Given the proximity to the busy street running above and behind the site, an apartment complex located to the east, and residences to the west, the desire was to be sheltered and protected from the surroundings. © 2004 Deborah Harde.

As seen from the southeast, the house and studio are a composition of five horizontal "landings" along the exterior stair. © 2004 Deborah Hardee

The concrete exterior stair terminates at the public entry, offering alluring views of the backyard area landscaped with native plants. © 2004 Deborah Hardee

The spaces within the residence are open to one another. The kitchen with its exposed concrete walls, a plywood and parallam stair, concrete and steel counters is located on the fourth/public level, which it shares with the bar, dining, living, pantry, and powder room. © 2004 Deborah Hardee

The guest powder room with a cantilevered concrete counter was designed to create a feeling of tranquility. © 2004 Deborah Hardee

The foundation and supporting structure of the residence are exposed within the internal stairway. The exposed foundation also serves as a frame for the occupants' modern art. © 2004 Deborah Hardee

The master bathroom offers a view to the outside yet provides privacy. © 2004 Deborah Hardee

At the highest level of the house, the fifth level, the major rooms are above the treetops, looking at the vanishing horizon of the desert and mountains beyond. © 2004 Deborah Hardee

Barn Beams and Modern Steel

The site is a dramatic seventeen-acre mountaintop property. Designed by R. S. Granoff Architects P.C., the house sits on a knoll at the highest point. Perched at the edge of a twenty-foot high retaining wall, it is an eclectic mix of old barn beams and modern steel detailing. The intricate lighting is high-tech. The "rustic" materials and finishes include reclaimed oak flooring, stacking stone veneer, and country tile.

The house, which resembles a modern barn, suits its mountaintop setting. It offers panoramic views of the countryside. *Courtesy of Elliot Kaufman Photography*

The architectural plan has a good deal of interest with the strong diagonal wall bisecting the house. *Courtesy of Elliot Kaufman Photography*

The open living/dining room permits wonderful parties. The old barn beams stand in splendor here. *Courtesy of Elliot Kaufman Photography*

The entry hall reaches for the stars.
Courtesy of Elliot Kaufman Photography

Granoff Architects designed the family room on columns (left) so that it floats above the landscape. *Courtesy of Elliot Kaufman Photography*

The gourmet kitchen has windows galore. Note the cabinet windows at the ceiling. *Courtesy of Elliot Kaufman Photography*

The mountains surround the eating area. *Courtesy of Elliot Kaufman Photography*

Through its ingenious structural design, Granoff Architects provided further views through the peaked ceiling family room. *Courtesy of Elliot Kaufman Photography*

The back staircase offers classic steps of beauty.
Courtesy of Elliot Kaufman Photography

Railing detail. Note the lighting. *Courtesy of Elliot Kaufman Photography*

The contemporary front staircase fades into the room. *Courtesy of Elliot Kaufman Photography*

Cliffside Villa

The original Colonial Spanish style home had graced the cliffs of Laguna Beach for over 40 years. It had become a community landmark.

Brion Jeannette's goal was to preserve the community's pleasure in designing the new home. He also wanted to create a home that would appear as if it had been on this prominent site for decades and that maintained old world charm while capturing the spectacular views.

Perched on a cliff in Southern Laguna Beach, California, the villa is a landmark property boasting creature comforts that exceed the imagination. The villa is the coveted location of philanthropic events and parties for the rich and famous. *Courtesy of Eric Figge Photography*

Brion Jeannette created an entry statement that compliments the importance of this villa. Roof eaves were given a genoise detail, mimicking a European villa. The entire lawn and entry gardens are actually roof top landscaping for the subterranean six-car garage and practice pistol range below. *Courtesy of Eric Figge Photography*

The entry foyer is marked by elegance and charm. *Courtesy of Eric Figge Photography*

Interior designer David Harte turned this wonderfully open kitchen plan into a delightful European country experience. Stone from old French chateaus grace the floors, and hand crafted tiles and marble adorn the counters. *Courtesy of Eric Figge Photography*

Harte visualized a formal design for the expansive living rooms separated by a grand marble dual fireplace. This Baroque style lends itself perfectly to the piano concerts cherished by visitors to the villa. *Courtesy of Eric Figge Photography*

Harte imported the best possible antiques to create an office that says, "Take me seriously." *Courtesy of Eric Figge Photography*

This lower level family room opens not only to the Pacific Ocean but also to the indoor pool and solarium. It is home to a stunning salt-water fish tank, majestic fireplace, and big screen TV. *Courtesy of Eric Figge Photography*

The solarium has an indoor swimming pool and swim-up bar. The room can be opened to let a warm summer day in or closed up to enjoy its pleasures all year long. A motion sensor activates the theme song from *Jaws* as soon as someone steps into the pool! *Courtesy of Eric Figge Photography*

The guest bathroom, as the entire house, has modern conveniences and state of the art technology, which is environmentally sensitive to energy conservation and green building materials. *Courtesy of Eric Figge Photography*

David Harte designed a whimsical and completely elegant master bedroom. *Courtesy of Eric Figge Photography*

The master bath emulates some of the most elegant baths in the world. Note the imported marbles and the faux painting on the ceiling. *Courtesy of Eric Figge Photography*

The fully mirrored exercise room takes you away from the present and charges you with desire for getting fit. *Courtesy of Eric Figge Photography*

Perched by itself on the bluff, the guesthouse boasts a hand crafted fireplace and full wall French doors that open to the gardens and Pacific Ocean views. *Courtesy of Eric Figge Photography*

Leaving the villa is not easy, but this view of the gardens outside the breakfast room (on the left) and the solarium pool room (below and center) is a memory not soon erased. *Courtesy of Eric Figge Photography*

High Desert

The driving concept for RKD Architects in designing this home was to create a relationship among the homeowner, architecture, and environment. The privacy, natural springs, creek beds, and uninterrupted views of a 13,000 foot Colorado mountain range made the apex of a high desert canyon ideal for the home site. Natural creek beds on the lot were supplemented to create tiered ponds and streams.

The home's design allows maximum connection with the environment. Angled glass bridges allow more outside windows and unobstructed views while spanning the water below and connecting three living "pods," which are nestled into the hillside.

Unconventional, contemporary curves and slopes are combined with traditional materials while battered, curved, and overhanging architectural forms evoke the geology. The occupants are sheltered yet a part of the landscape.

The home's massive stone forms appear to grow out of the canyon walls. Nestled into the side of canyon walls, three living "pods" are interconnected by angled glass bridges. The pods include the tower and guest pod with a crow's nest room reached by elevator or spiral staircase, a main living pod, and the master suite pod. *Courtesy of Ron Ruscio Photography*

Offering views of a private stream and pond below, this bridge of angled glass connects the main living pod to the private master suite pod. *Courtesy of Sally Brainerd*

The bridges in the home have angled glass to bring the outdoors in. *Courtesy of Sally Brainerd*

Stone and patinated copper used on the exterior carry to the inside to reinforce the connection to the site. The extensive stone also enhances the natural setting and grounds the home to its site with permanence. A subtle waterfall welcomes each person ascending the main stair to the primary living spaces. *Courtesy of Ron Ruscio Photography*

The great room area contains dynamic forms of copper and stone beneath a simple timber canopy. All of the living spaces open up to vast views of the surrounding rugged terrain. *Courtesy of Ron Ruscio Photography*

Stone and copper forms extend from the entry up into the living spaces above. *Courtesy of Ron Ruscio Photography*

The radial windows overlook red canyon walls and a pond below. Sloping window walls overhang the pond and stream below. *Courtesy of Sally Brainerd*

The kitchen is the centerpiece of the home. Walls of outward-sloping glass meet granite counters, which sit atop curved custom-built steamed beech cabinets. *Courtesy of Sally Brainerd*

Patinated copper forms one large wall of the kitchen and encases the stainless steel appliances, art display areas, and island. *Courtesy of Ron Ruscio Photography*

A separate pod contains the master suite. Canted, copper-clad window walls look out onto a private waterfall and walking paths. *Courtesy of Ron Ruscio Photography*

The bedroom and the bathroom share a two-sided fireplace. *Courtesy of Ron Ruscio Photography*

Clad in copper, these curved and sloping windows afford a view of dynamic red canyon walls and mountains. *Courtesy of Sally Brainerd*

Winterwood: An Ozark Estate

Hidden in the forest within the Ozark Mountains of Northwest Arkansas, just outside of Eureka Springs, sprawls Winterwood, an eighty-five acre lakeside estate. With six structures and more than three quarters of a mile of private lakeshore, this Adirondack-styled estate is reminiscent of the great camps that graced the woods of New York State in the early nineteen hundreds.

Winterwood includes the main building, the sleeping quarters, a bed and breakfast guest cottage, a lakeside summer kitchen, a lean-to, and a utility building that handles the estate's water, backup power, and communications needs. In true Adirondack tradition, each of these structures has its own use and is situated on the grounds to maximize its purpose.

After entering the grounds through a massive stone and wrought iron gateway, visitors pass a waterfall cascading off a natural Ozark limestone bluff before coming upon Winterwood Lakeside Cottage. Perched on the side of a mountain, the three-story cottage provides a breathtaking view of Beaver Lake, a 25,000 acre haven for water enthusiasts.

Its vaulted wooden ceilings, wood studded walls, and finished plywood floors highlight the main building. With its two gigantic stone fire places, leather furniture, Oriental carpets, and a collection of deer, moose, and bear heads that adorn its walls, the architecture and furnishings of the structure create a rustic and luxurious environment.

There are eighty-nine handcrafted stairs descending the mountainside from the main building to the suspension bridge that spans the brook cre-

The dogwood in full bloom adds its charm to this view. *Courtesy of Eric T. Schabacker*

ated by the waterfall. Once on the other side, a meandering boardwalk leads the adventurer through the forest to both the lean-to and summer kitchen.

One of the most interesting attributes of the Winterwood Estate is Winterwood Recording Studios, a state of the art digital audio facility located on the floor below the living area in the main building. Comprised of three recording rooms, a control room and musicians lounge, the studio attracts local and national artists, most of whom take advantage of the overnight accommodations. The studio's staff has been involved in more that 100 gold and multi platinum projects worldwide.

Seen from the main building, Winterwood Lakeside Cottage is perched on the side of a mountain overlooking a secluded branch of Beaver Lake. *Courtesy of Richard Leo Johnson/Atlantic Archives.com*

Leather sofas and Oriental carpets appoint the living room of the lakeside B&B. *Courtesy of Allen Smith*

One of the three cozy bedrooms at the B&B. *Courtesy of Allen Smith*

A lakeside boardwalk leads to the picnic grounds and dock. *Courtesy of Eric T. Schabacker*

Eighty-nine steps lead from the suspension bridge to the main building and sleeping quarters.
Courtesy of Eric T. Schabacker

The main building's living room replicates the wooden studded walls and truss work typical of the various structures on the estate. The huge, shaped tree stump table, trophy elk, and various other mounts and pelts lend themselves to the lodge feel. *Courtesy of Richard Leo Johnson/Atlantic Archives.com*

Where the action is — Winterwood Studios' control room. *Courtesy of Eric T. Schabacker*

The B Studio is one of three digital recording rooms at Winterwood Studios. *Courtesy of Richard Leo Johnson/Atlantic Archives.com*

Platinum records (awarded the staff at Winterwood Studios) accent twin Steinway pianos. *Courtesy of Eric Schabacker*

One of only a few rooms with a ceiling less than 26 feet high, the formal dining room was designed with intimacy in mind. A sixteenth century Italian mosaic depicting Christ's breaking of the bread heads the table. *Courtesy of Richard Leo Johnson/Atlantic Archives.com*

A Vermont Castings gas heat stove and lodge pole pine bed add warmth and elegance to the master bedroom. With its exposed truss work, the ceiling creates openness large enough for a wild bear! *Courtesy of Richard Leo Johnson/Atlantic Archives.com*

Afternoon shade provides relaxing views of Beaver Lake from the Winterwood Lakeside Cottage B&B. *Courtesy of Eric T. Schabacker*

Coming to life after a cold winter, one of three garden areas sets off the view of the oak-sided main building. *Courtesy of Richard Leo Johnson/Atlantic Archives.com*

A meandering stairway, known as "The Stairway to Heaven," leads to the suspension bridge, picnic grounds, summer kitchen, and lean to. *Courtesy of Eric T. Schabacker*

The Ultimate Bachelor Pad

The initial architectural challenge was to design a structure that the City Council and local environmentalists would approve and the owners would enjoy. The community did not want to lose the "rock form," a coveted landmark. Architect Brion Jeannette created the ultimate solution. The home built within the rock form creates an environmentally sensitive and energy-efficient solution that was eagerly embraced by the city and the owner.

Brion Jeannette's design removed the rock form interior, leaving the sides and top intact. After a concrete roof was poured, the original landscape was restored on top of the roof. Within the rock form is a wonderful 3,500 square foot home. *Courtesy of Eric Figge Photography*

Surrounded by rock formations, the dramatic entry with its waterfall feature welcomes visitors and minimizes the traffic sounds from the Pacific Coast Highway. Custom glass blocks were used to light the entry naturally. Stainless steel fascia and garage door are in contrast to the natural landscape. *Courtesy of Eric Figge Photography*

The whimsical and playful Gaudi-inspired interior features create a sense of wonder. Strategically placed skylights and fully opening glass walls wash the entire house with natural light. The entry waterfall feature can be seen in the rocky stream to the left. *Courtesy of Eric Figge Photography*

97

Terrazzo stone, complete with fossil shells, creates a dramatic kitchen and dining room floor. The entire ocean-facing glass wall folds away to reveal the delight of southern California coastal living. *Courtesy of Eric Figge Photography*

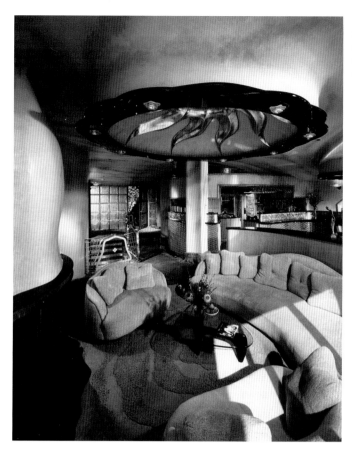

Designed for comfort, the intimate living room provides for casual living with a twist of intrigue. The glass walls can be opened completely to the outside patio and coastal views. *Courtesy of Eric Figge Photography*

The downstairs is designed to be the ultimate adult playroom with billiard table, bar, wine cellar, home theater, home office, and guest suite. *Courtesy of Eric Figge Photography*

The downstairs play area opens to the gracious lower level patio with spa, fire ring, and access to the beach below. It's an easy walk down the rock form stairs from the living level to the lower patio. Glass sections in the upper deck floor allow natural light in the lower level. Nature is the theme – it's everywhere. *Courtesy of Eric Figge Photography*

Situated on the edge of the rock cliff, this "bachelor pad" appears to be growing out of the rock. The roof is not only home to all the naturally existing vegetation but also the owner's vegetable garden! *Courtesy of Eric Figge Photography*

Curved Spine Organization

Moore Ruble Yudell had clients who wanted a house both economical and expressive. They sought the playfulness and sensuousness of curved forms both because of the wife's background as a modern dancer and for their energetic young sons. The resulting house combines the economies of large, simply enclosed loft spaces with the interior organization of a curved spine. Living spaces are organized along the spine and reach out into the landscape as limbs defining and flowing into intimate outdoor spaces.

The house is fit along the narrow portion of the lot. Entry is celebrated at the beginning of the spine. One slips through spaces that contract and expand vertically. The spine of the house terminates in a small garden sheltered by a tree canopy: a space of quiet and contemplation completing the mind/body duality.

The geometries and choreography of this house transform a simple loft typology into a richly woven hierarchy of places to move through and inhabit.

The house offers a view of the Pacific Ocean. *Courtesy of Kim Zwarts*

The entry. *Courtesy of Kim Zwarts*

The large central
gallery acts as the
focus of activity.
*Courtesy of Kim
Zwarts*

It connects spaces and paths vertically, linking horizontally to hillside and ocean-side gardens. *Courtesy of Kim Zwarts*

This seating is adjacent to the living room. *Courtesy of Kim Zwarts*

Upstairs the spine becomes a bridge between the children's and the parents' bedrooms. The bridge doubles as bench and library. A small study is tucked into a bay, which watches over the entry. *Courtesy of Kim Zwarts*

The bath. *Courtesy of Kim Zwarts*

Longview House

Joel Karr, architect, designed this luxurious house as a retreat and a family gathering place. Set on a secluded site in western North Carolina, the house commands dramatic views of the lake and surrounding mountains. Because of the slope, which is at a 30-degree incline adjacent to the lake and has clay-based and unstable soils, the site needed significant stabilization in the construction process.

The design theme makes use of the notion that a series of square forms, articulated by sloping roof forms and vertical "sail" elements, allowed the house to gently step side-wise down the slope, giving the interior spaces a gracious sense of descending from one end of the house to the other. This shallow stepping theme was a direct response to the concern of the owners about their own aging as they lived in the house.

Generous use is made of natural local materials and sustainable design precepts. The house uses copper roof sheathing, intended to patina and change over time, making the house an organic "living" work. Local shale stone is employed generously as wall and floor surfacing materials. Additional "green" concepts include deeply overhanging eaves shading generous south facing windows and double-glazing on all south, east, and west facing windows.

The house is sited on a secluded hillside in western North Carolina. *Courtesy of Jay Weiland*

The site required significant structural remediation in the construction process. *Courtesy of Jay Weiland*

A series of five square roof forms are articulated in copper sheathed planes, with vertical stone "sail" forms anchoring the angled planes. Each roof tilts up and out, allowing each interior space to open out to the views, creating dramatic interiors. Shaded north-facing patios buffer the driveway approach. *Courtesy of Jay Weiland*

The broad, curved deck provides a dramatic counterpoint to the angled series of square forms and the pointed roof corners. It steps down side-wise to respond to the slope. *Courtesy of Jay Weiland*

Deep overhanging eaves provide shading for the south-facing windows, while the deck itself also shades the rooms below, making this home very energy efficient. *Courtesy of Jay Weiland*

The square roof forms tilt up and out, to open each space to the spectacular view down the lake. Each of the roof forms is articulated by a square formed of glu-laminated beams. *Courtesy of Jay Weiland*

The kitchen and breakfast room enjoy the views of the lake. *Courtesy of Jay Weiland.*

The entry area is sheathed in local stone, with uplights washing through blind-mounted glass shelves. *Courtesy of Jay Weiland*

The master suite, located at the bottom, most secluded part of the house, includes his-and-hers closets and a sitting area. *Courtesy of Jay Weiland*

The master bath off the bedroom makes use of light and mirrors to allow the owners to have both a sink vanity and a make-up area, while including both a bathtub and shower enclosure in frosted glass. *Courtesy of Jay Weiland*

Contemporary Elegance on a Vermont Hillside

The clients lived in a traditional, dark, brick house in Georgetown, D. C. For retirement, however, they wanted a contemporary house to match their anticipated new lifestyle. This house is located on the edge of a traditional New England village. The house had to accommodate specific antiques, pieces of art, and a large Chinese tapestry.

BL Benn Architects organized the house on three levels: the entry/living level between guest quarters below and owner's suite above. The core of the design is a two-story great room that opens to a long deck and the panoramic views. The east wall is designed to permit natural light to penetrate deeply within the interior space.

When the house was completed, the owners expressed delight about the positive impact of the natural light on their spirits and how it allowed them to see the subtle beauty of their antiques for the first time.

The site slopes steeply down from the road with extraordinary views to the east across the Connecticut River Valley to a beautiful range of New Hampshire mountains. *Courtesy of Bernie Benn*

The house is organized on three levels: the entry/living level between guest quarters below and owner's suite above. *Courtesy of Bernie Benn*

Back to back fireplaces divide the great room from a formal sitting room. The sitting room contains the antiques and is designed to allow reflected sunlight to enter the space indirectly through inset baffled skylights. *Courtesy of Bernie Benn*

The core of the design is a two-story great room that opens to a long deck. The east wall is designed to permit natural light to penetrate deeply within the interior space. *Courtesy of Bernie Benn*

The natural illumination is soft, ample enough to show off the colors of the woods and inlays of the antiques, and diffused to protect the furnishings from fading. *Courtesy of Bernie Benn*

The Crest of the Hill

The client told Robert Oshatz, Architect, that he wanted a home that would be expressive yet nestle into its hillside site in a forested ravine. He was interested in using natural materials and blurring the line between interior and exterior. He wanted a home that he felt was a work of art, where he could enjoy a life of bird watching, music, and fine wines (built into the hillside on the lower floor is a 2,500 bottle wine cellar). To achieve this, he wanted an open plan with a main living space acoustically suitable for live chamber music and choral singing.

Robert Oshatz provided the acoustic sound desired through using curved Yellow Alaskan Cedar glue-laminated beams and a wood ceiling. Oshatz used red cedar walls, copper barrels, and glue-laminated beams to obscure the difference between interior and exterior.

The site is at its steepest on the south side where you get the full effect of the 20-foot cantilever of the living area deck. To provide privacy from the neighbors to the west, the deck curves up. *Courtesy of Meredith Brower*

When you walk around to the downhill sides of the house, you see that this two-story home stretches along the edge of a hill. Clad in cedar shingles, the lower floor is devoted to sleeping areas. The upper floor contains the garage, service entry, study, powder room, and living area. *Courtesy of Randy Calvert*

You drive down a 150-foot driveway to reach the home. From this view, it appears to be a small home with cedar shingle walls and a copper color mirror band above hiding a garage, some Alaskan yellow cedar beams leading to an entry courtyard, curving roof lines, and curved copper clad walls. *Courtesy of Meredith Brower*

To the right is the service entry and to the left is the powder room. The study is located in the center glass area. The circular groove under the roof overhang controls the flow of rainwater. *Courtesy of Randy Calvert*

Each bedroom and bathroom has a large view into the forest. The shingle walls and soffits continue into the interior, blurring the relationship between interior and exterior. *Courtesy of Randy Calvert*

As you turn into the Japanese garden, you see that the curved copper wall defines the entry area and continues its curving way into a fascia surrounding the courtyard. Eight-inch strips of copper color mirrors, which wrap their way through the entry and into the house, are between the copper and cedar shingles. *Courtesy of Meredith Brower*

The glass pivoting entry door defines the shape of the space. You can look through the tubular shape to the relaxation room and forest beyond.
Courtesy of Meredith Brower

This view from the entry looks back to the Japanese garden. *Courtesy of Meredith Brower*

The house was designed from the inside out. As you approach the house, you are introduced to a vocabulary of forms and materials that are reintroduced on the inside. *Courtesy of Randy Calvert*

Looking back at the house from the cantilever deck, you can see the small telescoping structure, which is the relaxation room. *Courtesy of Randy Calvert*

The relaxation room is a small space for reading, viewing, and relaxing. The room has sliding glass doors that partially go into the walls. *Courtesy of Randy Calvert*

As you leave the study, the view opens up to the main space of the house. *Courtesy of Randy Calvert*

The continuous south wall living area cabinet turns into a window seat at the fireplace alcove.
Courtesy of Meredith Brower

On the left of the walkway into the study is a light well for the hallway below. For safety reasons, 1/2 x 4-inch acrylic plastic strips are used. At certain angles, the strips resemble wire cables. The window is to the Japanese garden in the entry courtyard. Notice how the interior materials are woven with the courtyard materials.
Courtesy of Meredith Brower

Italian Hillside Villa

In the Los Gatos Hills perched up above the Santa Clara Valley in California is a 6,000 square foot home on an oak-studded hillside. Situated behind a private gated drive, the home designed by Debra Kay George Interiors is reached via a scenic creekside road through the hills. The three-level, five-bedroom, seven-bathroom home has valley views from the back and hillside views from the front.

The home is perched on the edge of a hill in Los Gatos. *Courtesy of Ken Huening*

The entry was designed to create a formal, yet inviting, living and entertaining environment, in a neo-classic style. *Courtesy of Ken Huening*

In the foyer, a two-story tromp l'oeil mural, custom painted by talented artist Jon Hunt, invites the guests to venture into the Italian countryside. The horse in the painting is actually the owner's, which personalizes the mural as well. An eighteenth century French antique Aubusson tapestry hangs on the stairwell wall. *Courtesy of Ken Huening*

Off the foyer is the formal living room, containing neo-classic furnishings. The windows are left unobstructed with simple shades so the view can be enjoyed and the architectural molding surrounding them appreciated. *Courtesy of Ken Huening*

Connecting with the living room is the formal dining room, allowing a nice flow while entertaining. An Italian import, the dining room table is made of a beautiful mahogany, with ebony inlays of flowers and swags. *Courtesy of Ken Huening*

To the left of the foyer is a hallway showcasing some of the owners' art collection. The art pieces are displayed on a heavy plaster, glazed, cracked-linen wall treatment, enhancing the old world appeal. An antique English mahogany long case clock, circa 1780, graces the end of the hall. *Courtesy of Ken Huening*

Rich burgundy colors add warmth and drama to the master bedroom. A leaf motif from the bedding was painted on the coffered inset in the ceiling, and the wall behind the bed is a mottled faux finish. *Courtesy of Ken Huening*

The large kitchen and breakfast nook has a wall of French glass doors, which exit onto a deck. Traditional cherry cabinets and blue fabrics create a slightly more casual space to relax or entertain. *Courtesy of Ken Huening*

The backyard is stunning with the pool's disappearing edge cascading water in a constant stream. It also contains a fountain, gazebo, outdoors kitchen, bar, and gardens and has breathtaking views. The multiple decks and large yard provide a wonderful space for entertaining large groups. *Courtesy of Ken Huening*

View of valley from back deck.
Courtesy of Ken Huening

Steep and Deep

Situated on a steep, dramatic site in the Rocky Mountains, this timeless residence, designed by RKD Architects, enhances the experience of living in a mountain environment by capturing and amplifying the benefits of the sun, views, and terrain, while still conveying a strong image of protection from the elements. Its organization entices visitors to enter through a composition of vertical stone monoliths. Above, the stone forms give way to horizontal elements, including concrete planes and horizontally banded zinc siding and fenestration, which reach out to the forest and views from the upper levels.

The house from a distance. *Courtesy of Monika Hilleary*

Approached from below, the home's initial image is twofold: the stone walls convey the strength of the building as it holds back the hillside, but the layering of the walls and the transparency of the living areas above invite the visitor indoors. *Courtesy of Monika Hilleary*

Full-height windows create a floating roof look, while corner glass allows panoramic views of nearby ski runs. Large roof overhangs allow sunlight in winter but provide a nice shield during summer months. *Courtesy of Monika Hilleary*

The master wing, shown here, is nestled into the hillside providing privacy and connection to the environment. A private deck rests against the aspen trees and natural vegetation. *Courtesy of Monika Hilleary*

The kitchen, great room area, and surrounding decks face to the west to capture dynamic mountain views and spectacular sunsets. *Courtesy of Monika Hilleary*

The entry of the home has 6-inch concrete stair treads, which cantilever from a curved, rose sandstone wall. The dramatic, floating staircase leads to the open living, dining, and kitchen areas above. *Courtesy of Monika Hilleary*

Upon arrival on the main living level, the vertical stone forms give way to horizontal elements that reach out to the environment. *Courtesy of Monika Hilleary*

Red sandstone carries from the exterior to the interior, connecting the natural site with the home's occupants. Horizontal slabs of concrete form floating planes within the home and extend beyond to the exterior of the home. *Courtesy of Monika Hilleary*

Cement, slab countertops, and stone floors provide strength and permanence to the kitchen while its high ceilings and windows provide a light and airy feel. *Courtesy of Monika Hilleary*

Bay Area Cliff Dweller

Avila Design built this 4,041 square foot house under a canopy of mature oak trees on a steep hill in the San Francisco Bay area.

The landscaped berm creates a natural transition from the upslope road and provides a green edge along the entrance walk. The glass-walled space in the foreground provides abundant north light into a spacious home office. *Courtesy of Avila Design*

The recessed and north-facing entrance is flanked with weeping bamboo landscaping and slate paving, which add texture to the refined lines and smooth exterior wall finish. A symmetrical, double door entrance is achieved by a "fixed" panel door to the left of the main door, which serves as its jamb. *Courtesy of Avila Design*

The entrance to the home opens directly to the living and dining rooms and the tree-studded hillside beyond. The illuminated wall niches frame the owners' sculpture collection. A cantilevered, granite-clad hearth extends the length of the millwork wall, providing overflow seating. *Courtesy of Avila Design*

A view of the dining area looking southwest. The steep downhill slope is approximately 20 feet below the level of the deck. *Courtesy of Avila Design*

This view of the living room from the dining area illustrates the relationship of the formal spaces and the kitchen area. Full height panels can be closed to provide visual and acoustic privacy. The uphill slope and landscaped berm adjacent to the front entrance provide enough privacy to eliminate the need for window coverings at the front of the house. *Courtesy of Avila Design*

The kitchen is flooded with tree-filtered natural light by full-height east and south facing window walls. The pantry is strategically placed between the sink counter and stair that leads to the lower level garage. The pantry can be closed from view by the pocket door just visible at the right hand side of the counter. A generous butcher-block table extends the island and provides a pleasant place for the owners and guests to enjoy light refreshments. *Courtesy of Avila Design*

There are symmetrical outdoor decks on either side of the dining area. Mature oak trees and decks to accommodate outdoor dining surround the dining area. This west-facing view shows the deck leading to the master bedroom at the far west side of the home. *Courtesy of Avila Design*

This more than utilitarian stair leads to the garage and lower level game room and visitor quarters. The frameless corner glazing seen at the intermediate stair landing window wall is a feature used throughout the home. *Courtesy of Avila Design*

The reading room on the main level of the home is a soothing space. The large oak trees on the south side of the property and operable windows provide shade and allow cool coastal breezes to provide thermal comfort on the occasional hot days in the Bay Area.
Courtesy of Avila Design

The lower level entertainment center also serves as visitor's quarters and has a separate bath, closet and outdoor deck. *Courtesy of Avila Design*

This view from the intermediate landing of the internal stair highlights the exacting level of detail and indoor/outdoor space manipulation required. *Courtesy of Avila Design*

The site slopes 12 feet across the footprint of the house designed by Stevens Architect. *Courtesy of Ross Chandler*

3.

On the Hill

Cliffhangers stand on hills, mountains, and cliffs. Hopefully, the architect has considered the topography, the landscape, the climate, and those all-important views in siting the house. Often, the plan has to address environmental challenges affecting construction costs, neighborhood resistance, and sightlines designed to preserve neighbors' views, weather, and agency regulations governing development. Certainly, steep sites present more difficulties than horizontal ones, but they present possibilities for exciting resolutions.

House/Site Integration

The clients for this custom residence wanted to build a spacious, light-filled timber frame home with craftsman roots that took full advantage of their secluded property just south of Bellingham, Washington, and its spectacular views. Precipitous slopes of sandstone dotted by colorful Madrona trees and blankets of Salal distinguish the site. Fir-covered mountains form its backdrop, the San Juan Islands its horizon. These elements were central to the conception of the design and its development.

Zervas Group Architects gave careful attention to complementing the natural features of the property and integrating the house into the site. To this end, they took two approaches: one was to build into the existing cliffside, making the landscape part of the architecture; and the other was to perch the structure above the grade and let the uneven surface slip beneath and away from it.

The first approach was achieved by means of an organically shaped, stone "outcropping" that emerges from the site's steep contours and anchors itself to the earth. This "landscaping" element carries lichen-covered ledgestone into and through the house, adding color, texture, and a sense of permanence. On the first floor, the outcropping contains the garage, mud/laundry room, part of the master suite, and a sunroom for growing plants. The sunroom also separates the public and private sides of the house and is open to the stairs that lead to the open loft above. At the top of the stairs, one can access the flat-roofed "outcropping," which provides an outdoor patio garden in lieu of a traditional yard. Its tip offers views down the cliff side and out to the islands; its surface blends back into the sandstone, blurring the boundaries between built and unbuilt.

Intersected by the "outcropping" are two, pitched timberframed structures that represent the second approach to siting the home. The larger of the two contains the bulk of the public domain and is open in plan between the kitchen, living, and dining rooms and in section to the loft above. The building also opens itself to the exterior with large expanses of glass and generous decks that feel like outdoor rooms. Different layers of views through the house and out to the landscape, water, and islands beyond are achieved by opening the floor plan and stepping its profile on the exterior.

A smaller timber structure is tucked away on the other side of the "outcropping," which contains the master bedroom with a private deck that looks down into a sheltered cove. A passage through the stone wall opens to the master bathroom and leads to the mud/laundry room and back into the entry foyer or out to the garage. The suite is organized and situated on the site to feel like an intimate, private domain while remaining open to its surroundings.

Aside from stone, wood is the most prominent material both inside and out. On the interior, the Douglas fir timber frame sets the scale and rhythm of the spaces, and the building is detailed to emphasize its structural role as well as its natural beauty. The walls were painted off-white to emphasize the timbers' rich color, and windows are expressed as openings between structural posts and beams as opposed to punched holes in a wall. Cherry flooring and casework add warmth and complement the timbers as well as the colors found in the stone masonry.

The house perched on the sandstone bluff of Chuckanut Bay opens itself to the exterior with large expanses of glass and generous decks. *Courtesy of Doug J. Scott/dougscott.com*

On the exterior, a steeply pitched, stepped gable roofline is the most dominant feature of the home when viewed from the approach. Its cedar shingle roofing has quickly weathered to a soft gray, not unlike the color of a typical day in the Pacific Northwest. *Courtesy of Doug J. Scott/dougscott.com*

The house is a part of its site. The deep red window frames echo the papery bark of the Madrona trees. *Courtesy of Doug J. Scott/dougscott.com*

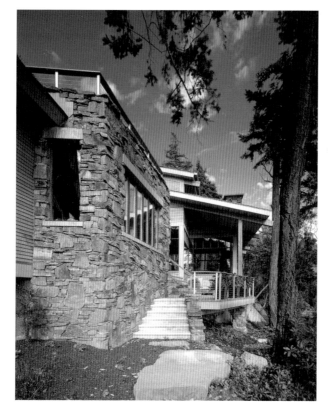

The ledgestone masonry was chosen to reflect the diversity of colors, tones, and textures that make up this very northwest scene. *Courtesy of Doug J. Scott/ dougscott.com*

Soft, mottled toned slabs of limestone are used in the entry foyer for the flooring, while the ledgestone that can be seen on the exterior of the home is also featured here. The Douglas fir car decking that is used for the floor of the loft above can be seen as the ceiling of the entry foyer. *Courtesy of Doug J. Scott/ dougscott.com*

The walls were painted off-white to emphasize the rich color of the Douglas fir timbers, and windows are expressed as openings between structural posts and beams as opposed to punched holes in a wall. Cherry flooring and casework adds warmth and complements the timbers as well as the colors found in the stone masonry. *Courtesy of Doug J. Scott/dougscott.com*

The Douglas fir timbers are evident throughout the house. *Courtesy of Doug J. Scott/ dougscott.com*

The kitchen features large expanses of black granite countertops and plenty of storage. The dining room is separated from the kitchen by a built in buffet. *Courtesy of Doug J. Scott/dougscott.com*

Island Residence

The steep, two-acre island site is located on one of the highest points in the area. Stelle Architects' site strategy was to create a semi-public space on the east or street side. On the west side, they maintained existing vegetation around the private pool and terrace area, creating a "treetop" like presence with views in all directions.

The design strategy organizes a series of private and semi-private spaces around a main living, kitchen, and dining area. The separate volumes are clearly delineated by their materials, colors, textures, and intersections. They are connected with a transparent, finely detailed glass and metal structure housing the communal space.

The architecture attempts to achieve a greater understanding between the relationship of the building to its environment through tectonic clarity, sequence, and order. Inside and outside spaces are interconnected and unobstructed, creating fluid spaces and reinforcing the building's relationship to its site.

The house has commanding views of the surrounding bays, islands, Long Island Sound, and distant Connecticut shoreline. *Courtesy of Jeff Heatley Photography*

Sitting on the terrace, you have 180-degree views. *Courtesy of Jeff Heatley Photography*

Dining here is a pleasure. *Courtesy of Jeff Heatley Photography*

If the sun is too much, you can retreat to the inside but still enjoy the scenery. *Courtesy of Jeff Heatley Photography*

The living room in this 3,000 square foot house is expansive. *Courtesy of Jeff Heatley Photography*

The kitchen is a chef's dream. *Courtesy of Jeff Heatley Photography*

Even the master bath has incredible water views. *Courtesy of Jeff Heatley Photography*

The lavatory has its spot of beauty.
Courtesy of Jeff Heatley Photography

Windows and stair details
work together. *Courtesy of
Jeff Heatley Photography*

The Cabin

"It was like being hit by lightning," according to the clients, who had been given 113 acres in Montana's Judith Mountains. The land already had a small log cabin on it. Located at the very bottom of the canyon, in a grove of old firs, it was always dark, cold, and claustrophobic. The clients desired light, sun, and expansiveness.

A forest fire that burned across part of the land in 1989 exposed just such an opportunity for Jeff Shelden of Prairie Wind Architecture. Sited about 70 feet above the valley floor, on the edge of a limestone ledge, the site with its long views up and down the valley seemingly hangs in space. But, it also has the intimacy of an aspen grove and a meadow of wildflowers.

The client also wanted the cabin to relate to their cultural landscape as well as the physical one. Raised with both the myth and reality of the great Western forests, he wanted a place where life and relationships were condensed to their essential elements, where nature overwhelmed and embraced those lives.

The cabin had to become a part of those landscapes. It also had to look old from the moment it was finished. To accomplish this, Shelden used a lot of recycled material.

View of the cabin from the southwest corner. *Photo by Lois Shelden*

View of the cabin from the east, with the composting toilet enclosure in the foreground. *Photo by Lois Shelden*

View from the south, with the hillside sloping away to the north and west. The wood-fired hot tub is in use. *Photo by Lois Shelden*

The upper level provides the connection to the views with windows in every direction and a 6-foot square skylight at the peak of the roof. *Photo by Lois Shelden*

Ground floor interior shows the antique Hoosier cabinet and sink base cabinets. The Hoosier has been wired for lights, and the sink has running water, courtesy of the photovoltaic panels and a solar-powered well pump. The woodstove colors helped determine the interior finish colors. *Photo by Lois Shelden*

On the second level. there is also sleeping for two and storage. *Photo by Lois Shelden*

Ground floor interior image shows the finishes and furniture, including a futon for sleeping and a built-in antique corner cupboard. *Photo by Lois Shelden*

The second floor interior storage, lined with aromatic cedar for the bedding, is in the foreground. *Photo by Lois Shelden*

Crescent-Shaped Hillside Home

The site for this home designed by Anderson Anderson Architecture is a steep, south-facing hillside with panoramic views overlooking Puget Sound, the city of Tacoma, and Mount Rainier. To either side are neighboring houses looking directly across the site, diminishing privacy and affecting the pristine 180-degree sweep of dramatic distant views. To accomplish the clients' objective of maximum privacy and open the house with an uninterrupted glass wall, the firm decided upon a semi-circular plan. This half-donut shape with a solid wall to the outside and a glass wall on the inside creates privacy for the house and deck.

The structure takes on a crescent shape through the offset radii of two intersecting arcs, which form the structure and enclosure of the building. This offset resulted from the need for a larger space at the main living area and smaller space requirements at either end of the circle, where a bedroom and a music room are located. Although the plan was best accommodated with a crescent shape, the roof structure was far more economical as a simple, semi-circular structure of identical, equal bays.

The differential arcs of the roof and the enclosing wall below are also situated for optimal sun shading. The two arcs are most nearly tangent at due south, where the incoming sunlight is most vertical. The arcs diverge, creating deep overhangs towards the ends of the crescent and providing greater shading for more horizontal sunlight in morning and evening.

A service wing extending back into the hillside serves to tie the building to the site and allows the main crescent shape to remain as one continuous open space subdivided and defined only by freestanding sculptural/functional elements such as the kitchen and the stone fireplace. At the intersection of the main crescent and the service wing, a four-story tower serves as the main entry. Twin studies capture spectacular marine and mountain views.

Designed and built for clients retiring from careers in the wood products industry, the structure and finishes of this house serve to showcase the technological and creative possibilities of the use of wood on a dramatic and challenging cliffside site. The crescent form was chosen to maximize views and privacy for the main living spaces and the courtyard deck, drawing on the inherent strength of its curved back shear wall to permit a completely open floor plan and uninterrupted glass curtain wall.

Sweeping curve of the roof and deck.
Photo by Anderson Anderson Architecture

156

Sweeping curve of the roof of the house in the evening. *Courtesy of Eric Browne*

Panoramic view of Puget Sound from the living room. *Courtesy of Eric Browne*

Kitchen with main living space beyond. *Courtesy of Eric Brown*

Main living space looking back across the deck to master suite. *Courtesy of Eric Browne*

Kitchen and deck from main living area.
Courtesy of Eric Browne

Llamas on the Hill

This hillside home, designed by Stevens Architect, is a response to the dichotomous set of desires of the client. On one hand, the client wanted to capture the warmth of the old family home in the Midwest. The ancestral home had been a series of dark, wood-trimmed, cellular-type spaces. On the other hand, the client wanted openness and irregular spaces. In fact, the client wished to have no rectangular or square living spaces.

The plan evolved as a response to the client's desires and the topography of the site. The hillside building asked for the house to be anchored on the windswept site. The site commands a 270-degree view from Mt. Bachelor in the west, Mt. Adams in the north, and the Ochoco mountains in the east. These view directions gave rise to the trapezoidal form of the living spaces. On the south side of the masonry wall, which anchors the house to the hillside, the service spaces of the residence are formed as regular utilitarian spaces.

The site slopes 12 feet across the footprint of the house. The main deck off of the living, dining, and office spaces cantilevers out over the slope. Under the cantilever, below the living space of the house is a storage area.
Courtesy of Ross Chandler

The view from the deck includes one of their two llamas. *Courtesy of Ross Chandler*

The entry way shelters incoming guests. *Courtesy of Ross Chandler*

The living space has an attractive angularity. *Courtesy of Ross Chandler*

The dining room continues the angular
theme. *Courtesy of Ross Chandler*

The kitchen makes entertaining easy.
Courtesy of Ross Chandler

The master bedroom connects to the lower deck and hot tub via an exterior spiral stair. *Courtesy of Ross Chandler*

Even the master bath has distant views as does the master bedroom. *Courtesy of Ross Chandler*

Homes that in the daylight have views for hundred of miles become glowing forms in the night that can be seen for miles. *Courtesy of Ross Chandler*

40-Degree Slope

This single-family building has 1,700 square feet of livable space in three stories with a 400 square foot garage. In undertaking this speculative project, Ming Lee, Architect, explored a standard approach to residential design on bay area hillsides, seeking to address inherent challenges such as site difficulties affecting cost of construction, growing neighborhood resistance, and stricter agency regulations governing development on hillsides.

The city guidelines called for articulation in architectural features and massing that step with grade, essentially de-emphasizing bulk that may be apparent from a distance. Destruction of the hillside's oak trees was discouraged; the lot sloped downhill at approximately 40 percent; and it was one of the smallest at a little under 5,000 square feet with adjacent buildings encroaching into property lines.

Lee's solution is a compact, simple offset of two rectangles that avoided the demolition of a mature oak tree at street front and nestled within the perimeter formed by four other existing oak trees on site. The offset also results three-dimensionally in what the city was looking for in an approvable design, stepping not only in profile but also in plan.

The same offset differentiates the living room from the dining-kitchen space without separating them and results in continuous yet unique spaces. A

One of the preserved oak trees embellishes the entry approach. You can see the different levels of the house to the left. *Courtesy of Amey Bhan*

ceiling height increase at the living room perceptively opens the space up and out beyond shoji-like, glass mall sliders that lead to the outdoor living room that is the balcony. This openness adds another 400 square feet of perceptible square footage to the living room. The experience from this space is akin to being in a tree house: you are high and above amongst oak trees that are just beyond your grasp.

The same diagrammatic rectangle translates into a compact solution of three bedrooms and two baths on the third floor that accommodates ideally a small starting family. In detail, elements such as thin cable rails, thin aluminum trims, glass guardrails, and open riser staircase are utilized to give transparency and allow flow and continuity of space. Windows at transitional spaces provide for surprises by framing native oak trees and distant lush hillsides beyond.

The cedar garage door faces the street. *Courtesy of Amey Bhan*

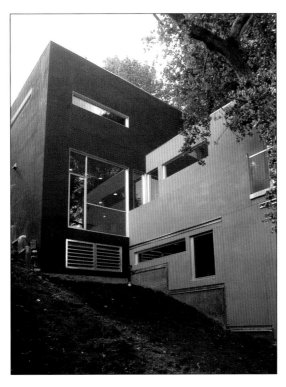

The view from the rear yard reveals an austere structure in contrast to the unassuming street façade. *Courtesy of Amey Bhan*

The centerpiece of the living room floor is an open riser staircase. *Courtesy of Amey Bhan*

The larger than typical laminate glass backsplash gives a gem-like luminance to the kitchen. *Courtesy of Amey Bhan*

At the entry, windows frame snapshots of nature beyond. *Courtesy of Amey Bhan*

The slate countertop island with the glass hood gives way to the living room, a wood-burning stove, and the vista beyond. *Courtesy of Amey Bhan*

The expansive mirrors in the bathroom reflect yet-another view of nature. *Courtesy of Amey Bhan*

The deck rail meets the kitchen window in a bold geometric intersection. *Courtesy of Amey Bhan*

The cedar deck and glass rail expand the interior living to the natural world. *Courtesy of Amey Bhan*

A Baja Cliffhanger

Todos Santos, Baja California Sur began to grow in the late 19th century, when sugar mills opened and merchants built handsome, tall windowed homes. Today, it is a quiet paradise, despite the transformation of some older buildings into handsome hotels and the loving renovation of the beautiful old buildings in the historic district by Americans who have made their homes in Todos Santos. Also, it has evolved with the presence of internationally known artists who have come to live there, tourists who revel in the area, and a surfer population who dwell around some of the world-famous surf breaks. There are about a dozen art galleries, but the town retains the feeling of a Mexican village with its crowing roosters, wandering cows, its rutted dirt roads, colorful bougainvillea, and rustling palms.

The owners run an eco-adventure tourism company. They had the help of an architect in designing this home.

This cliffhanger with its thatch roof and its brown terrace nestles among the giant Cardón cactus, the jumping cholla, yuccas, and mesquite. *Courtesy of Robert D. Evans*

The approximately 1,700 square foot house is open to the outdoors and the water. *Courtesy of Robert D. Evans*

It looks over a sweeping Pacific beach where the local fisherman cast their nets in the early morning and sea turtles return each year to lay their eggs. *Courtesy of Robert D. Evans*

The owners can marvel at the cavorting whales, listen to the whistling osprey, and watch the pelicans sweep in for fish. *Courtesy of D. Peter Lund*

The house embraces the lovely Baja climate. Consequently, it seems much larger than it is. *Courtesy of Robert D. Evans*

The fish tank is inserted into the wall of the great room. The owner built the fish tank himself! *Courtesy of Robert D. Evans*

The first floor master bedroom is open to the sound of the ocean. The bedroom is the only room in the house without a thatch roof because "the bugs can occasionally jump down"! *Courtesy of D. Peter Lund*

With its own entry, the office is also on the first floor. The Cardón skeleton is used to support the bookshelf. *Courtesy of D. Peter Lund*

The view from the top of the stairs. *Courtesy of D. Peter Lund*

The kitchen cupboard panels are made from the native Palo de Arco branches and Mexican pine. *Courtesy of Robert D. Evans*

Throughout the house, concrete is used for its coolness. It can be found on the kitchen counters and bar, stairs, bedroom floor, bed base and side tables, dining room floor, bathroom counters, great room sofa base and end tables, and office desk. *Courtesy of Robert D. Evans*

The dining room is open to that wonderful Baja environment. Every night the homeowners can dine to the sound of the rustling palms and the distant roar of the Pacific. *Courtesy of D. Peter Lund*

The column material for the dining room is made from the native strangler fig, which wrapped itself around the palm. Ultimately, the fig killed the palm. *Courtesy of D. Peter Lund*

The house features a palapa roof made of thatched palm fronds. *Courtesy of Robert D. Evans*

In the Puerto Vallarta style.
Courtesy of Robert D. Evans

Immediately outside the home is the garden. *Courtesy of Robert D. Evans*

And of course there are those Pacific sunsets – with the occasional green flash! *Courtesy of Robert D. Evans*

Among the Birds

This cliffhanger sits in its own aviary, which has been fostered for years by its owners: a dentist who loves ornithology and his artist wife. Foxes walk down the paths, woodpeckers rap on the trees, the Canada geese swim, and the chipmunks play among the budding rhododendron. As you walk in the scenic woodlands and admire the natural rock gardens of ferns, you can hear the waterfall, the bird songs, and the scurry of small animals. A flyway for many bird species, this quiet oasis offers peace and the quiet of the woods.

The house hugs the rugged New England cliff. *Courtesy of D. Peter Lund*

Its profile remains low. A balcony runs its length. *Courtesy of D. Peter Lund*

The great room is dominated
by the world outdoors.
Courtesy of D. Peter Lund

The artist's studio has great light. *Courtesy of D. Peter Lund*

And space for dreaming.
Courtesy of D. Peter Lund

Some formal plantings. *Courtesy of D. Peter Lund*

A beautiful sentinel. *Courtesy of D. Peter Lund*

And the house watches over it all. *Courtesy of D. Peter Lund*

The gorgeous wetlands.
Courtesy of D. Peter Lund

Canyon Site

The owners appreciated the modern values of openness, transparency, light, and simplicity but were skeptical of a preconceived aesthetic. AAA, a California-based architecture office, developed the resulting design in response to the owner's needs and values, including their desire to place the main living spaces on the top floor to take advantage of the view.

The site is in a small canyon at the base of the San Gabriel Mountains in Pasadena, California. The two previous houses on this site were destroyed by fire. The most recent fire in 1993 left a substantial concrete foundation (on a 40-degree slope) that became the starting point for this project. Today, the home responds to its hazardous setting with automatic fire sprinklers and fire-resistant exterior finishes.

The house was divided into three architectural components to reduce bulk and to create a dynamic and complimentary relationship with its natural setting. A solid stucco base rises from the existing foundation as an outcrop from the ground. The interior component of the house is a composition of wood floors and white walls that make up the house within. Wrapping most of the outside is a red, corrugated fiber-cement shell that provides fire protection and visual articulation. Almost all windows occur in gaps between these pieces.

The canyon's beauty conceals the threat of landslides, earthquake, flash floods, and fire. Here, you can see some scars from the 1993 fire that destroyed many homes. *2002 Erich Koyama*

The house is entered from the side on the lower level. A balcony and wall of windows with views up the canyon to the San Gabriel Mountains are above the balcony. *2002 Erich Koyama*

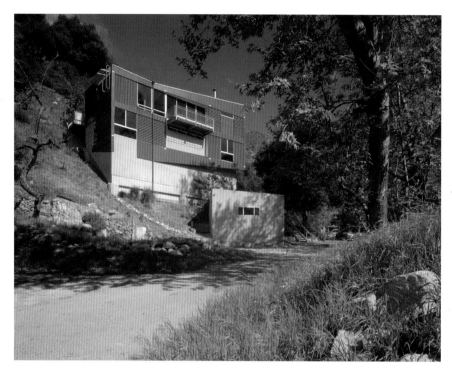

Both the house and garage were built upon the foundations of an earlier residence. The red "shell" wraps around the house to visually break up its bulk and pull the house closer to the ground. *2002 Erich Koyama*

A wood and steel stair conducts visitors directly to the upstairs living spaces. A red tile wall rises up to the second level alongside the stair. *2002 Erich Koyama*

The upper floor level is a large open room subtly demarcated into different spaces by material changes and other architectural elements. The entry stair arrives behind the living room. Large glass doors open to a steel deck that is set below the level of the floor. Lowering the deck prevents the guardrails from blocking views of the San Gabriel Valley. *2002 Erich Koyama*

The dining space enjoys generous views of the mountains. The material palette includes maple floors, unpainted steel, anodized aluminum windows, and pegboard cladding. *2002 Erich Koyama*

Steel rod X-bracing economically braces the window wall against earthquakes. A small balcony opens off of the dining space to the left. Natural ventilation through doors and windows prevents excessive cooling costs. *2002 Erich Koyama*

Leaving the kitchen open to the rest of the floor requires the space to be visually simple. The red tile backsplash is a continuation of the tiled wall of the entry stair. *2002 Erich Koyama*

Dramatic Solution to Steep Site

"Maine is a visual experience," says Donald Mallow, Architect and painter. The coast, especially at low tide, the blueberry fields with their scattered boulders left after the last Ice Age surrounded by hundreds of acres of low bush wild blueberry plants, brilliant red in September and October, the changing light and weather have been the material of his watercolors, pastels, and drawings for years.

He built a 2,700 square foot (exclusive of basement and attic) post and beam house, using common spruce and native cedar and, where necessary, engineered lumber for framing. His site was a steeply sloping wooded shore off the Salt Pond fed by Blue Hill Bay through an inlet and reversing falls between Mill Island and South Blue Hill Neck.

Working on a steep rocky site presented many considerations including the driveway design, tree preservation so to maintain sloping soils, design and siting to use the slope to its best advantage, location and grading of septic system, and disposal of the blasting debris.

There was also an issue of timing. The site was terraced early in the project since the construction of the septic system would prevent later access to the areas to be terraced. Many of the large granite boulders were found about five miles away; each stone was measured for size, fit, and orientation. Gradually, each stone found its place, and the fill brought in behind them shaped the nine gently ascending terraces as they are today. The stone retaining walls extending outward and downward from the building tie the building to its site.

The steep slope is terraced, using boulders, in conjunction with outcropping ledge, to create nine meandering retaining walls. Large boulders were fit together to form a base for the house anchoring it to the site while reducing an otherwise high aspect of columns and foundation. *Photo by Don Mallow*

The form of the upper roof begins as a gable roof, transitions to a hip roof, and completes as a gable to the ridge. *Photo by Don Mallow*

The 18-foot wide bay window looks out on the waters of the Salt Pond 50 feet below. A correspondingly wide portion of the ceiling is raised to 10 feet for musical acoustics for practicing, coaching, and rehearsing chamber music in this combination living/music room. *Photo by Don Mallow*

The north-facing studio has steady light and view of great boulders left behind at the end of the last ice age. *Photo by Don Mallow*

A local shop made the custom maple cabinets. The floor has a ceramic tile border at work areas and is oak at dining area for warmth under foot and a quieter floor. The bay window has built in counter with drawers, where the architect can listen to the morning news while his wife works at other counters. *Photo by Don Mallow*

The porch evolved from a screened porch to a space surrounded by casement and awning windows. When open, the windows create a screened porch that increases the length of seasonal use of this unheated space. *Photo by Don Mallow*

White cedar timbers and gravel form steps, which follow the downward outcropping ledge and glacial boulders. *Photo by Don Mallow*

The view from the balcony. *Photo by Don Mallow*

Vernacular Style: Energy-Efficient Cliffside Residence

This AIA award-winning house is situated on a small lot in an established neighborhood with houses of mixed architectural styles. The southern half of the land has a wooded ravine with a major drainage channel traversing its length, while the other half was very steep. The site presents open space and panoramic views to the west; the access is from the east.

The design by BL Benn Architects accommodates the needs of two career professionals and their two children. Zoned for privacy and acoustics, the house includes a separate entrance for a professional studio and a safe, level driveway. Energy efficiency, natural light, ventilation, and ease of maintenance were high priorities, but so were spatial delight and aesthetics.

This house and studio are constructed with an energy-efficient exterior shell and hot water radiant heating system. Gypcrete slabs over wood framed floors not only provide mass for the heating system but also control transmission of sound between levels. Super insulated exterior walls with an additional 3/4 inch reflective interior airspace not only provides high thermal efficiency but also gives the house a soft acoustical quality. Moisture and air quality are controlled with a whole house heat exchange ventilation system. A composite slab structure in the garage, a copper standing seam roof, stained cedar clapboards, and tile floors insure low long term maintenance

The site is organized with public access from the east and privacy to the west. Most spaces have southern and western exposure, while the northern exposure is limited. The approach to the house is through a landscaped courtyard with a roadside hedge for privacy and a formal planting of linden trees.

The garage door has an applied horizontal trellis to add to the "garden" courtyard aesthetic. *Courtesy of Bernie Benn*

Visitors enter the house via a bluestone walk and exterior gallery on the north. The studio is entered through an interior gallery to the south. The driveway, parking, and garage are located level with the roadway. *Courtesy of Bernie Benn*

A two-story porch dominates the west facade of the house. Views vary with the level and season, from shaded tree top vantage in summer to open panorama in winter. *Courtesy of Bernie Benn*

The house is vertically organized to step down with the natural grade to a walkout basement 3-1/2 floors below. Each level has either deck/porch or on grade access to the exterior. *Courtesy of Bernie Benn*

The living area entry has skylights and panoramic views at the top level. The open stair risers help to visually connect spaces. *Courtesy of GBH Photography*

Organized on half levels, the house moves easily down from the primary living space with its massive fireplace. *Courtesy of GBH Photography*

The sunspace and kitchen are open to the natural light.
Courtesy of GBH Photography

A two-story porch overlooking the valley dominates the west facade of the house. The porch provides sheltered outdoor sitting from the top-level living room and a cathedral deck space from the kitchen and dining level. *Courtesy of Bernie Benn*

Mt. St. Helens and Mt. Hood Views

Driving along the street, you might think the houses were built on standard suburban flat building lots. But once past the garages, the lots slope steeply down into a forest ravine. The clients had the steepest (i.e., 30-degree) lot in this subdivision and wanted an affordable starter home that would be ready in time for the arrival of their first-born child. Designed by architect Robert Oshatz, the house is a three-story, 1,925 square foot structure. Sloping slightly down from the street is the two-car garage and an entry area. From the entry, you can go down two-thirds of a level to the recreation level or one-third level up to the three bedrooms, two bathrooms, and a computer alcove. The top level is the living, dining, and kitchen area with another deck cantilevering into the ravine.

Affordability was the main criterion in selecting materials. To help control cost, the clients and their friends did part of the rough framing and finish work.

Above the two-car garage is a roof terrace, the equivalent of the old fashioned front porch, with a magnificent view of Mt. Hood. The exterior is made up of dark green sheet metal and a unique blend of copper color sheet metal and wood strips. *Courtesy of Randy Calvert*

As you turn into the driveway, you see the full play of exterior materials. The roof wraps into the diagonal soffit, creating a diamond shape upper living and kitchen level. The rectangle window framed by vertical wood strips and a copper color sheet metal panel represents the bedroom level. Below is the recreation level. *Courtesy of Meredith Brower*

From the side, the 30-degree slope of the ground can be seen. The vertical, two plus story shaft supports the diamond shape upper level with its projecting fireplace. The upper level is above the adjacent neighbor's roof and offers a view of Mt. Hood from one window and Mt. St. Helens from the other. *Courtesy of Meredith Brower*

From the forest ravine below, the vertical nature of the site and house is obvious. The lower recreation level has a wine cellar, powder room, laundry room, and a large recreation room, with a deck cantilevering into the ravine. Above is the bedroom level. *Courtesy of Randy Calvert*

The entry is a three-story light shaft with a staircase that leads to all levels. *Courtesy of Robert Oshatz*

As you enter the upper level, you have the kitchen to your left and living area to your right. Straight ahead are the dining area and a sliding glass door to the cantilever deck. *Courtesy of Robert Oshatz*

The upper level is one large open space. The kitchen has a center island, eating bar, and a "V" shape rear wall with a large working counter and a pantry cabinet on one side and a built-in seat matching the living area window seats on the other side. *Courtesy of Meredith Brower*

The living area side is centered on the fireplace. The large glass expanses define the diamond shape. Mt. St. Helens is to the left, and Mt. Hood to the right. Each alcove created by the roof overhang has a built-in window seat. *Courtesy of Meredith Brower*

Bernie's Castle

In the late 1920s, this hillside home was an 18 x 20-foot beach cabin on a 'tent-lot' high on the bluff above the Oregon ocean-front. Over the years, the base-ment was enclosed, a porch was added and then enclosed, and bedrooms and a potter's shed were added. By the time the home became Bernie's castle, seven 'tent-lots' were combined into one, and Bernie's dream of living in a lighthouse was created through the addi-tion of a tower.

After seventy years, the cur-rent owners saw potential in the decrepit shanty and called upon architect Cynthia Bankey to help them revive the home. They di-vided the floors into separate rental units, each with unique balcony and "lighthouse" features, and achieved an English Cottage look for the exterior with the addi-tion of a sloped roof and natural finish cedar-shake siding.

Upslope side of house after renovation into the English Cottage style.

Ocean side of house showing original three-story tower, additional new tower feature, and balconies.

Main unit living room from kitchen.

Main unit cottage kitchen.

Upper level of "lighthouse" tower feature.

Main unit family room.

Oceanside rock formations watch over the home.

Sunny Bay Residence

This house designed by Anderson Anderson Architecture is a set of three structurally simple shed or gable roof rectangles arranged in a rectilinear pattern and then set into a complex site. Multiple overlapping legal setbacks from the shoreline, the property lines, the natural runoff, the septic system, and other factors overlay the site with a complex multi-angled grid of limitations. In addition to these legally defined setbacks are the sightlines identified to preserve the neighbors' views, setbacks to preserve tree roots and existing site structures, height limitations to bring sunlight into the central courtyard at critical times of the day, and the desire to shield this central outdoor space from the prevailing afternoon winds.

The site is long and narrow with the narrow end facing directly south onto the beach with a 180-degree view from Mt. Rainier at the East to the Southernmost Olympic Mountains at the West. Rockeries and plantings as well as a roughly circular grove of 200-year-old Douglas fir trees surrounded the former buildings on the site. The natural and human-made conditions of the site had established wonderful outdoor spaces and patterns of use that had considerable meaning to the clients.

To preserve the existing trees required largely limiting new construction to the existing building excavations. The new and larger building is inserted so as to maintain the existing topography. Only one tree was removed to make way for the new house, and this large, twin-forked Port Orford cedar became the important structural column at the center of the new home. Surrounding greenhouses, docks, bulkheads, and other structures were repaired as necessary and maintained to preserve the rich texture of human activity on the site built up over many years.

Looking up to the house from the beach.
Courtesy of Michael Scarbrough

Side entry to the house. *Photo by Anderson Anderson Architecture*

Main living area with "column" constructed from a tree removed for the house building. *Courtesy of Michael Scarbrough*

Main living area as seen from master bedroom balcony. *Courtesy of Eric Brown*

Main stair to bedrooms. *Courtesy of Michael Scarbrough*

Alaskan Hillside

The smell of campfire smoke, the sound of glaciers cracking and popping, and salmon that arrive in waves all summer long: Alaska is an adventure. It is here that rivers are born, that humpback whales play, and eagles swoop. It is also here, just as in the lower 48, that a Timberpeg house can be built.

This Juneau, Alaska, home demonstrates that timber frames can be built almost anywhere. *Courtesy of Rich Frutchey*

The lot was extremely overgrown and incredibly steep; however, the owners wanted to take full advantage of the breathtaking panorama of local islands and surrounding cove. *Courtesy of Rich Frutchey*

The dramatic window wall in the great room brings the outside beauty inside for enjoyment year round. *Courtesy of Rich Frutchey*

Located in such a foggy and often cloudy location, this home's open floor plan and timber frame design allow abundant natural light to flow throughout every room. *Courtesy of Rich Frutchey*

The open galley style kitchen shares views with both the living room and dining area. *Courtesy of Rich Frutchey*

Unique and cozy, a balcony overlooking a great room is the perfect place for an office, library, or even a simple sitting area. This balcony allows the homeowner to take further advantage of the large great room windows. *Courtesy of Rich Frutchey*

The patio doors, windows, and skylights flood the master bedroom with light. The private deck features a commanding view of the sound below. *Courtesy of Rich Frutchey*

Hillside Renovation

Originally, this house was designed by a locally famous architect J.H. Thomas and built in 1914. Peter Brock, Architect, converted a formerly uninhabited "basement" space to a home office facing the front yard. The firm also remodeled the kitchen and added a new breakfast bay on the ground level facing the hillside at the back of the property. The upper level has great views of the San Francisco Bay and the Golden Gate Bridge.

Berkeley's sunny hills are home to dozens of handsome and practical homes by locally famous architect John Hudson Thomas, whose designs moved from the picturesque craftsman style to the more severe modernist lines of this 1914 example. *Courtesy of Peter Brock Architect*

The kitchen nestles into a compact sculptural garden cut into the uphill side of the site. A new large breakfast bay opens through unconventional open-corner casements echoing the house's original early modernist features. *Courtesy of Peter Brock Architect*

The breakfast bay straddles interior and exterior, providing a sheltered sunny eating spot that brings the garden inside when its huge corner casements are flung open. *Courtesy of Peter Brock Architect*

Ample counters at varied heights comfortably accommodate numerous cooks and modes of cooking. The split-level island screens the cooking area from view, displays the fancier serving dishes, and provides a long serving counter. *Courtesy of Peter Brock Architect*

A large secondary sink and copper-lined planter anchor a satellite cooking area at the north end of the kitchen. Ingenious fir paneling completely conceals the built-in refrigerator at the right. *Courtesy of Peter Brock Architect*

A new art glass skylight suffuses the central stairwell with daylight. The glass is supported on stained fir frames that incorporate the house's signature, four-square window mullion motif into a swirling pinwheel. *Courtesy of Peter Brock Architect*

The new bath annexed small amounts of space from two adjoining rooms and unified it under a long vault that extends the volume of the room to the back wall of the shower stall. New windows and a skylight combine with a mirrored wall to brighten and expand the space. *Courtesy of Peter Brock Architect*

Laurel Hill

Rural Berkshire County in Massachusetts has always appealed to those who want that idyllic spot. Over the decades, many have chosen to build homes here and to enjoy the cultural and recreational activities of the Berkshires, which range from skiing to fishing to classical music.

A retired pilot and his wife built a 6,000 square foot hillside home with the kitchen as the center.

The house looks south down the Housatonic River valley. The unusual rooflines add interest.

The house faces south, which gives ample radiation heating in the cold Massachusetts winters through the glass windows and door.

This view from the kitchen looks to the stone floor-to-ceiling fireplace in the family room.

From the master bed you can look at the mountains, the valley, and the sky.

The 8-foot glass window in the kitchen frames the rock garden to the rear.

The gourmet kitchen is indeed the heart of the house, making entertainment of friends and family a delightful experience.

Imagine looking at the stars from this deck.

At the Bottom of the Canyon

Positioned at the foot of a 100-foot wooded canyon is a house designed by Graymatter Architecture. The firm drew upon the topology to create an outdoor living room sculpted by the landform that borders it. The outdoor living room is bordered by indoor living space that opens to the outside in a myriad of different ways: a sloping retaining wall lined with fireplace, grill, waterfalls, and an ochre plastered fence wall with randomly placed openings through which passersby can peak in. The rear border is a wooded hillside with winding landscaped pathways leading upward.

The house is a microcosm of California, changing from the hard urbanity and warm beach climate of Los Angeles to a redwood hillside. At the street, it transitions from a tight urban street to a walled courtyard, which leads past a glass corner and waterfall /concrete pond. Turning the corner is the outdoor room with furniture designed in the same wood and plaster materials and vernacular as the house. From indoors, the views of the outdoor spaces are featured like a filmstrip through different types of opening: slits, a glass corner, sliding barn door, and pivot doors. Views up the hillside are framed as art by steel girders and wood doors in the main living space.

An entry gate leads to outdoor living room.
©2003 Grey Crawford

When seen from above, the house is only a silvery form within a wooded canyon. ©2003 Grey Crawford

The entry yard looks toward the pond.
©2005 Kenneth Ho

Steel channels in living room ceiling lead to
pitch of the roof. ©2003 Grey Crawford

A glass corner opens up living space to the outside with view of the pond. ©2005 *Kenneth* Ho

Tapering steps lead up through a sky lit void to the master suite. ©2003 Grey Crawford

Scrap lumber is compressed and used for stair treads and kitchen cabinets. ©2003 Grey Crawford

Here, you see the living room from the kitchen. ©2003 Grey Crawford

The bedroom is immersed in the verdant green hillside. ©2005 Kenneth Ho

The master bedroom has a custom bed with TV. ©2003 Grey Crawford

The dressing area has custom clothing storage. On the other side of the wall behind the bureau is the shower. ©2003 Grey Crawford

The west has many exciting houses. *Courtesy of Paul Doherty*

This house, designed by Robert Oshatz, clings to a 30-degree slope rising above the Willamette River with a spectacular view of the river, Mt. Hood and rising sun. *Courtesy of Robert Oshatz*

The site is a 23,000 square-foot lot, sloping up from the street. The house is a three-story structure with each story being a split-level for a total of six levels. *Courtesy of Robert Oshatz*

4.
Free Spirits

Frank Lloyd Wright said, "Architecture is life or at least it is life taking form and therefore it is the truest record of life as it was lived in the world yesterday, as it is lived today, or ever will be lived." *An Organic Architecture MIT 70*

California Hill House

Sited on a ridge top, ten miles from the Pacific Ocean, the Hill House is often buffeted by winds of more than 100 miles per hour. The house, designed by Jersey Devil, a nomadic group of design-and-build architect contractors, is cut into the crest of the ridge to present a low profile to coastal storms. It sits in a south-facing bowl encouraging the wind to pass over while still allowing for generous sunlight.

By following the contours of the ridge and using earth berms, stone from the site, and a living roof, the house blends into the natural terrain. This strategy provides fire, wind, and earthquake resistance as well as reducing heating and cooling loads. Thermal mass construction and earth integration help to mitigate temperature swings.

A Trombe wall that operates by convective loop is 60 percent below floor level to allow for direct gain view windows above. The wall curves from south to southwest, and its passive solar components (glass, concrete, metal) contrast with softer, more natural forms and materials of the east and north sides (earth boulders and fieldstone). A windmill pumps water to a storage tank, and the water is gravity fed to the house. Domestic hot water is solar heated.

A bird's eye view from the south. *Courtesy of Bob Easton*

Aerial view from the west. *Courtesy of Bob Easton*

Even in the summer, the Hill House is always cool— thanks to its buried form. *Courtesy of Steve Badanes, Jersey Devil Architects*

The organic sensibility of this residence can be seen in this view from below. *Courtesy of Steve Badanes, Jersey Devil Architects*

The sod roof is apparent in this view. *Courtesy of Steve Badanes, Jersey Devil Architects*

There is an excavated entry courtyard and cave-style garage. *Courtesy of Steve Badanes, Jersey Devil Architects*

The entry is covered. *Courtesy of Steve Badanes, Jersey Devil Architects*

Michael Moore did the painting; John Kapel, the table. *Courtesy of Steve Badanes, Jersey Devil Architects*

The master bedroom has a curved vanity leading to the master bath. *Courtesy of Steve Badanes, Jersey Devil Architects*

The headboard is cast in concrete. Jim Adamson's light fixtures incorporate backlit foam nerf balls in concrete culverts. *Courtesy of Steve Badanes, Jersey Devil Architects*

The kitchen and living area. *Courtesy of Steve Badanes, Jersey Devil Architects*

The kitchen. *Courtesy of Steve Badanes, Jersey Devil Architects*

The Snow Clam

Two brother carpenters, who just happened to own a truckload of redwood siding, asked Robert Oshatz, Architect, to design a house for one or two families at a 10,000 foot elevation. From the front door, you can ski down to the ski lift!

A central shaft running vertically through the house supports the three floors and provides each floor with its own fireplace. The house has two garages, one on each side of the entry. When you enter the house, a half level down takes you to the family areas. A half level up takes you to the master bedroom suites (each suite is separated by the central shaft) with a fireplace and whirlpool situated within the shaft area. The lowest level is a children's playroom and dormitory. Oshatz designed the undulating roof to recall the mountaintop behind the house. Local residents refer to the house as the snow clam.

The street level entrance and flanking garages are on a split-level on the uphill side. A copper panel separates the custom redwood entry door from the clerestory windows. To minimize the garage doors, they are clad, as is the rest of the house, in tongue and groove redwood siding. *Courtesy of Tom Church*

The house stretches from the street to the beginning of the Aspen grove. The redwood siding creates patterns of vertical and horizontal lines, leading your eye around the numerous elements of the house. *Courtesy of Tom Church*

From the lower side of the hill, you can see the central structural shaft growing out of the ground. The shaft elevates the lower level windows above the winter snow— a typical problem for houses in the area. Looking up, you can see the children's circular lower level and the middle level deck cantilevering out to the trees. *Courtesy of Tom Church*

From the split-level inner entry, you can see the river stone circular central structural shaft. The staircase leads up to the two master bedroom suites. The clerestory windows flood the entry with morning and late afternoon light. *Courtesy of Howard Alan*

The middle level of the house meets the Aspen grove at the cantilever deck, which wraps 180 degrees around the house. *Courtesy of Tom Church*

A whirlpool and fireplace separating the two master bedrooms is in the center of the structural shaft on the upper level. You can sit in the tub and stoke the fire! *Courtesy of Tom Church*

From the whirlpool, you can look through the large arched window to the Aspen grove. *Courtesy of Tom Church*

Each master bedroom is circular in plan with a large arch window focusing on the mountain peaks. *Courtesy of Tom Church*

The middle level living room is a semicircular, partially two-story space centering on the fireplace. *Courtesy of Howard Alan*

The kitchen area is well appointed. *Courtesy of Tom Church*

The lower level children's playroom is a semicircular area centering on the fireplace in the central structural shaft. The continuous window ledge holds mattresses and sleeping bags for guests. *Courtesy of Howard Alan*

Multipurpose Cabin

The Tomahouse Bale Classic is a building of the future, a multipurpose cabin, which can be adapted to any number of situations and environments. Using patented German technology by PT BPT BaliClavis, the modular building system can be customized to suit a wide range of applications.

The revolutionary design is based around a rigid aluminum skeleton, which creates the core structure of the modular building. Each interlocking meter-square panel is fastened to the adjoining sections by a patented locking system, simple enough for a child to assemble and yet robust enough to withstand extremes of external pressure.

Once the basic floor plan is in place, the chosen living or working environment can be created from an extensive selection on ancillary modules. Because it is modular, simply purchasing more modules and connectors can expand it.

The TomaHouse at night is a lovely sight. *Courtesy of Moch. Sulthonn and Aji Mahareshi*

Its lightweight aluminum structures, designed and fabricated in Germany, are transportable anywhere in the world. The living room in a TomaHouse is truly elegant. *Courtesy of Moch. Sulthonn and Aji Mahareshi*

The master bedroom is modern and yet cozy. *Courtesy of Moch. Sulthonn and Aji Mahareshi*

Utilizing natural elements such as wood, rock, and natural fibers, the Toma combines German technology with the charm of Balinese craftsmanship. *Courtesy of Moch. Sulthonn and Aji Mahareshi*

The shower. *Courtesy of Moch. Sulthonn and Aji Mahareshi*

Toma on the rocks. *Courtesy of Moch. Sulthonn and Aji Mahareshi*

243

Football House

Near the San Andreas Fault in a northern California redwood stand lies a guest-house/study addition known as the Football House. Instead of disturbing the redwoods, the Jersey Devil designer/builders, Steve Ba-danes and Jim Adamson, used a truss bridge to connect the old with the new.

Perched on a 45-degree slope, the addition is pinned to the ground by two concrete piers sunk into the hillside. Rising from the piers are two wooden frames, to which are attached two, lenticular or football-shaped trusses that act as bearing walls with floor decks and roof spanning between. The frames end in a pyramidal skylight.

The significant slope to the site was one of the primary reasons for choosing these trusses. The house, which is an addition to an existing residence, is a study or guest quarters for the main house. A deck on the downhill side has a magnificent view of the redwoods. Inside is a two-level guest room and study— finished by the client— with a ceiling that follows the football's upper cover.

The house is poised above a 45-degree slope. *Courtesy of Steve Badanes*

View from the east. *Courtesy of Steve Badanes*

The bridge connection to the existing house. *Courtesy of Steve Badanes*

Detail of the connecting bridge framing.
Courtesy of Steve Badanes

View downhill is from the northeast. *Courtesy of Steve Badanes*

The ceiling of the interior is gently curved. *Courtesy of Steve Badanes*

Peter Whiteley designed the entry door. *Courtesy of Steve Badanes*

The redwood trim is slender; all workspaces, cabinets, and bookshelves are built in. *Courtesy of Steve Badanes*

The redwood deck provides spectacular views. *Courtesy of Steve Badanes*

The Bird House

Originally designed and built as a speculation project, this house was based on a cross-axial plan centering on a direct view of Mt. Hood, approximately 50 miles to the east. On the minor axis is a band of clerestory windows, which admit natural light into the main living levels of the house. The cross-axis sits on a vertical shaft that rises out of the ground, eliminating the need for a pier foundation system, which is common in neighboring houses.

From the street, the house, designed by Robert Oshatz, is entered via a bridge, which doubles as the carport. The bridge springs from the hillside, anchoring the house and giving reinforcement to the horizontal aspects of the design. Tall shafts of fir trees and the main massing of the house itself give the composition a strong interlocking counterpoint to the design and an anchor to the steep site. The locals call this residence "The Bird House."

A two car carport and entry walk lead to a private entry courtyard. The structure appears to spring from the street and bridge across to a vertical shaft. *Courtesy of Robert Oshatz*

The large cantilever of the street floor balcony can be seen from the down hill side of the house. Notice in the corner where the balcony and shaft meet how the beveled cedar siding changes direction to accentuate the house lines. *Courtesy of Robert Oshatz*

Close up. *Courtesy of John Fulker*

The kitchen is a two-story volume. The diamond window above with its wrought iron pattern on the exterior side shares its light with the master bedroom dressing area above. The window in front of the sink has blinders on the outside that block the view of the neighbor's house. *Courtesy of John Fulker*

Staircase from master bedroom suite. *Courtesy of Robert Oshatz*

From the dining area can be seen the two-story volume living area, a cozy area centering on the fireplace. The diamond window above the fireplace shares light with the master bedroom above. *Courtesy of John Fulker*

The master bedroom is an attic-like space that looks through a triangular opening to the diamond window and living area below. Through the French door is a small balcony. *Courtesy of John Fulker*

The 5 x10-foot window provides another picture perfect view of Mt. Hood.
Courtesy of John Fulker

The whirlpool tub permits summer breezes and views of Mt. Hood.
Courtesy of John Fulker

A Geodesic Dome

Domes have been around for centuries. Think about those cathedrals. Even our ancestors knew that domes could enclose the most volume with the least surface. Geodesic domes use self-bracing triangles in a pattern, which distributes the loads throughout the structure, thus giving maximum structural advantage.

Noted architect Buckminster Fuller proved that geodesic domes get stronger, lighter, and cheaper per unit of volume as their size increases – just the opposite of conventional buildings. Reinforced concrete dome home shells are able to withstand enormous wind and snow loads and are fully capable of supporting earth beaming.

An American Ingenuity dome is purchased as a shell kit. Purchasers without prior construction experience can build their own dome, or an independent subcontractor can assemble the dome shell. The simplified building process consists of placing a row of panels, overlapping and interlocking the steel mesh from adjacent panels, and filling the seams with a specially formulated concrete.

High vaulted ceilings are a natural for domes. The strength of the dome is sufficient to suspend the second floor, eliminating the need for load bearing walls, and allowing for large open floor areas. Reduced surface area, uninterrupted insulation, lower air infiltration, and expanded polystyrene (EPS) insulation four times thicker than that used in refrigerators provide savings in heating and air conditioning cost that often exceed 50%.

The dome nestles into the hillside. *Courtesy of American Ingenuity*

The skylights provide abundant natural lighting for the home. Two layers of thick tempered glass make the skylights strong and energy efficient. Cupolas provide lighting and ventilation and may offer a third floor loft with a 360-degree view. *Courtesy of American Ingenuity*

The view from the bottom. *Courtesy of American Ingenuity*

House in Rockscape

Barrett Studio Architects' "House in Rockscape" is an experience of rock, sky, and distant vistas. It is both a sanctuary and an atmospheric observatory. As home for a couple, a scientist and a fiber artist, it is a blending of technology and art, masculine and feminine, earth and sky.

The site, located in the foothills of the Rocky Mountains, is a spectacular geological event. The granite promontory upon which it sits juts out from the side of the mountain over a steeply sloping valley below. Just as a lizard suns itself on a rock, the house is an organism touching down lightly in the granite pile — while opening itself to sun and views. All mechanical systems are contained in the underbelly, in lieu of excavation that would have disturbed the delicate ecology of this place. The entire elevated steel structure rests on just six piers that are anchored into bedrock. This system allows the house to be a delicate addition into the natural vocabulary of the site. The result is an elevated structure intertwined with rocks, trees, and sky.

This aerial photo shows the home's relationship with the landscape. *Courtesy of Aero Arts Photography*

Here, the blending of the materials palette and color scheme with indigenous rock is evident. *Courtesy of Aero Arts Photography*

The custom deck is an example of the indoor/outdoor living emphasized in the home's design. *©Ronforth/Ronforthphoto.com*

The valley spread below the "prow" of the deck. ©Ronforth/Ronforthphoto.com

An interior entry. ©Ronforth/Ronforthphoto.com

The interior finishes emphasize a connection with the natural world. ©Ronforth/Ronforthphoto.com

An interior doorway. ©Ronforth/
Ronforthphoto.com

Even the bar is unique! ©Ronforth/Ronforthphoto.co.

Imagine enjoying that
cool frosty drink from
here ! ©Ronforth/
Ronforthphoto.com

Unicorn Farm. *Courtesy of Joseph Henry Wythe*

Details. *Courtesy of Joseph Henry Wythe*

The entry. *Courtesy of Joseph Henry Wythe*

5.

The Creation of Unicorn Farm

Joseph Henry Wythe

When the Wythes decided to return to the north country of Idaho, Joseph made an expedition there to determine the best place to relocate his architectural practice. After selecting Sandpoint, Lois went up to search for the ideal site where they could construct their home and studio: a place on a lake, river, stream, or pond where they could watch wildlife come to the water.

Experiences with the local real estate salespeople were quite amazing. One day, Lois found herself in the office of a young salesman who was the first and only one who appeared to be doing things right by inquiring in detail about the kind of property desired. In observing that about every third vehicle was a big pickup with a gunrack in the back window, Lois was somewhat shy about letting her inquisitor know that they wanted to establish a wildlife sanctuary. Consequently, her responses to some of the questions were a bit evasive. "Yes, we are looking for rural property where we will be doing some farming."

"But what are you going to raise on your property?" he repeated.

After dancing around that inquiry several times, Lois finally replied, "Well, I'll tell you what. We're going to raise unicorns."

"Oh!" he responded as he began flipping through the pages of his listing book. "In that case, you will need a property with a high fence around it."

When Lois reported on her expedition, she remarked that "I haven't found our property, but I know what it's going to be called."

Unicorn Farm was built in a magical sort of forest of larch and cedar bordered on two sides by the river. Upon entering the forest, one is aware of the spirit of place as the driveway curves through the trees, never allowing a straight shot view of the site. This gives a sense of mystery that is maintained as one approaches the dwelling — especially in moving through the interior spaces.

In the heart of the forest is a clearing with a hill sloping toward the south to a serene, natural, spring fed pond — a place where Joseph and Lois could watch unicorns and other wild creatures come to the water — and an ideal site for an earth-sheltered dwelling. To better observe the scene, Lois wanted all windows to be bay windows.

The heart of the home is the large kitchen where Lois prepares her gourmet vegetarian cooking. The large, center island, with its laminated wood top for chopping vegetables, is covered with all manner of produce in season, herbs, and other delights. She can look up into the trees above the six-foot square skylight, which can be raised for ventilation. Between the ovens and the antique wood range is the baking center with its low height countertop of laminated wood and small garages for mixers and other equipment.

The kitchen commands a view into the living and dining areas of the great room and on out into the screened porch. The open, hooded fireplace can be seen from all portions of the room. The hexagonal alcove of the lounge area with its built-in seating gives a sense of intimacy but not isolation from the larger space. Near the great room are the studios — one where the herbal newsletter *Lines From Lois* is written and the other for the creation of works of architecture.

The fireplace can be seen from the lounge, dining room, and kitchen. *Courtesy of Joseph Henry Wythe*

The great room. *Courtesy of Joseph Henry Wythe*

The kitchen. *Courtesy of Joseph Henry Wythe*

Since the dense stand of larch trees in the forest needed thinning, a logger set to work cutting selected trees, skidded the logs with a team of beautiful draft horses to his portable mill near the building site, and sawed the logs into the boards and timbers used for the framing and roof deck. After the lumber was dry, the framing was constructed. 2x6-inch boards set on edge and nailed together were used for the roof deck, providing a beautiful ceiling and adequate support for the weight of the structure, 18 inches of wet earth, plus the heavy snow loads. Heavy retaining walls of concrete and stone resist north and west earth pressures, while protected wood framing is used

on the berm walls below the windows. Waterproofing, insulation, and earth were placed over the roof and walls, leaving only the doors, windows, and skylights exposed to view.

The house can be easily be heated by the fireplace and three wood stoves, using the abundant fuel available from the forest. The primary source of heat, however, is a water source heat pump operated air conditioner. Even when the pond is beneath a foot of ice, energy is transferred from the water in the pond to coils at the bottom and circulated to the heat pump. The system can be reversed to provide cooling during the occasional hot periods in the summertime. (A

kitchen refrigerator is really a small heat pump.)

Although this mechanical system is very energy efficient, the major conservation comes through the careful attention to providing a building envelope that effectively resists the migration of heat from or into the dwelling. Thick layers of polystyrene insulation are placed below the concrete floor and cover the roof deck and retaining walls, including the bermed walls under the windows. Fiberglass insulation is also packed into the 10-inch stud spaces around windows and doors. An air door test was made to detect excessive amounts of heat loss resulting from air seeping through walls, electrical outlets, spaces around doors and windows, and other openings in the envelope. Doors and windows are thoroughly weather-stripped. The casement windows use multiple layers of glass and argon to increase energy efficiency. Heavy, wool shades that coil under the windowsills can be drawn upward to provide additional insulation at the windows; they can be raised to the desired height to eliminate the sun's glare or ultraviolet light while still providing views to the outside.

The governing order of the plan is established by the use of angles based on multiples of 22 degrees. thus 45, 90, degrees etc. The plan is arranged to provide for a sense of mystery as one moves through — the unfolding of dramatic vistas — the desire to explore spaces that are suspected but not seen around the next corner — the surprising discovery of new delights. The impact is enhanced by the space flowing out from under low soffits up into the higher ceilings and recesses above.

The home is an expression of Wythe's architectural philosophy - human scale, space modeling, the continuous present, a symphony of materials, at one with its surroundings. Inside, one is hardly aware of the home being buried into the earth; it is delightfully open to the outside world. Not requiring the heavy construction to resist earth loads, the screened porch sweeps delicately out towards the pond. The home blends naturally and harmoniously into its site.

The studio. *Courtesy of Joseph Henry Wythe*

The master bedroom. *Courtesy of Joseph Henry Wythe*

The master bath. *Courtesy of Joseph Henry Wythe*

Hillside architecture can mean minimizing the presence of the building to preserve the view. Here, on this site just below Mount St. Helena in Sonoma County, California, the red building will be replaced. *Courtesy of Kathy Shaffer Architecture & Design*

Building A Hillside Home

Kathy Shaffer

The selection of an architect is crucial when building a hillside house. By working closely with an experienced architect, you can identify, refine, and ultimately build the best solution for your project.

A hillside site for your home offers numerous opportunities that a flat site cannot. Improved sun angles provide more interesting light and play of shade and shadow. The dwelling can be tucked into a shaded side of the hill for a cooler, peaceful effect with diffuse light and muted colors, or it can be sited on a southeastern-facing slope to maximize the pattern of the sun and provide bright natural light and intense colors.

Most often, a hillside site presents the opportunity for a view. In urban settings, now more than ever before, neighbors on opposing hills with a view of your home must be respected. More towns are requiring that new construction minimize glazing to reduce glare, use darker colors to blend in with the landscape, and reduce the mass of a building. In response to these new codes, manufacturers are slowly beginning to develop more affordable products that respond to these requirements.

This building designed by Kathy Shaffer is proposed to replace the red building. The use of porches and an outdoor pool terrace provide a leisurely setting for enjoying the views. *Courtesy of Kathy Shaffer Architecture & Design*

This 1960s home in Mill Valley, California, was designed for a flat lot and adapted to the hill by placing it on piers and posts. The owner requested Kathy Shaffer Architecture & Design create a new design that would increase views, bring more sunlight into the home, and have the style of an Italian Renaissance villa. *Courtesy of Kathy Shaffer Architecture & Design*

To garage.

VERSION B

-fire resistant
  -tile roof
  -stucco
- scale / mass / height
  -minimal overhang
  -varied planes

The proposed design by Kathy Shaffer changes the style of the home and opens up the back of the home with decks, windows, and porches in order to maximize the view. The design follows the topography of the hill and provides small terraces to stabilize the hill. *Courtesy of Kathy Shaffer Architecture & Design*

North elevation and color scheme. *Courtesy of Kathy Shaffer Architecture & Design*

The south elevation looks toward the view. *Courtesy of Kathy Shaffer Architecture & Design*

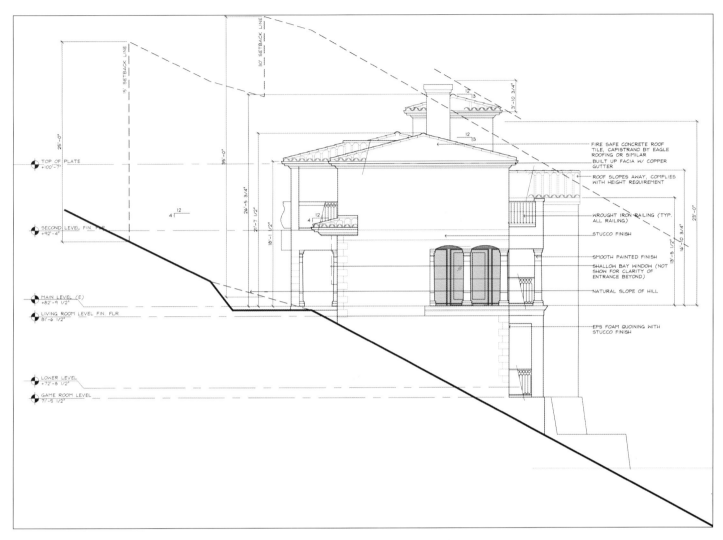

Windows and openings are minimized to maintain privacy from neighbor and reduce solar heat gain. *Courtesy of Kathy Shaffer Architecture & Design*

Finally, a hillside home provides the opportunity to integrate the house into the hill. This theory of organic architecture, whose most noted advocate was the architect Frank Lloyd Wright, in essence proposes that the house merge with the hill. This task can seem daunting, requiring structural engineering, civil engineering, soils analysis, and more. If careful steps are taken, however, close work between the architect and these consultants provide the opportunity for improved privacy and reduction of the visual mass of the house. Rather than perching a house on a lot, for example, the home can be built into the side of the hill, giving the appearance of cascading down the hill. In this way, the dwelling contributes to the appearance of the hill and gives it character and appeal.

Resources

Architects and Designers

AAA is a small California-based architecture office interested in creating high quality modern design. AAA believes that Modernism is not a style, but a set of values that places quality and performance above trendy novelty or escapist fantasy. They are committed to pursuing this ethic to create architecture that is engaging and appropriate to our age. Their office brings experience, energy, and creativity to any project.

150 Haight St.
San Francisco CA 94102
415.626.6499
www.aaaarch.com

Anderson Anderson Architecture is a diversely experienced firm with a strong foundation in construction practicalities. As designers of award-winning modern homes and buildings in the United States and Asia, the firm offers new technology, environmental integration, design excellence, and value. The firm's comprehensive services integrate creative architecture, planning, landscape, and construction consulting for diverse project types.

90 Tehama St.,
San Francisco, CA 94105
415.243.9500
83 Columbia St., Suite 300, Seattle, WA 98104
206.332.9500
www.andersonanderson.com

Next generation architecture describes the innovative architectural firm of **Avila Design**. The firm believes that the twenty-first century must signal a renewed design approach while paying respect to the past. It specializes in unique solutions to residential, retail, and commercial projects with its practice built on thoughtful and uncompromising dedication to design excellence. The firm continually evaluates its work processes and implements new ways of problem-solving.

436 14th St.
Suite 1123
Oakland, CA 94612
510.893.2000
www.aviladesign.com

Steve Badanes is part of a loose-knit group of designer-builders, known as Jersey Devil, who have created projects that critique conventional practice, both the process of making architecture and the accepted definitions of architecture itself. Their architecture shows a concern for craft and detail, an attention to the expressiveness of the construction materials, and a strong environmental consciousness. All the members of Jersey Devil teach at the Yestermorrow Design/Build School in Warren, Vermont, Steve Badanes also directs the Neighborhood Design/Build Studio at the University of Washington in Seattle.

The Yestermorrow Design/Build School
189 VT Route 100
Warren, VT 05674
802. 496.5545
888.496.5541
www.jerseydevildesignbuild.com/about.htm
designbuild@yestermorrow.org
online.caup.washington.edu/courses/
hswdesignbuild

Cynthia Bankey Architect, Inc. has been in operation since 1991. The goal of her firm is to provide high quality design, balancing the practical and the artistic elements of buildings into a coherent vision. Elements of sustainable design are incorporated in each project, including low toxic materials and methods, water- and energy-conserving strategies, and emphasizing human friendly spaces and amenities without compromising clients' financial goals. The size of the firm permits flexibility in client base and design opportunities.

2115 SE 46th Ave.
Portland, OR 97215
503.294.7912

Sears Barrett Architects state that their goal as residential architects is to discover and give form to the unique aspirations of its clients. Their design-oriented approach encourages client collaboration in shaping dwellings that benefit the land and the client. The firm believes that an artfully crafted residence can contribute directly to the client's experience of living well.

7901 East Belleview Ave., Suite 250
Englewood, CO 80111
303.804.0688
www.searsbarrett.com

Through the expressive use of alternative and sustainable materials, **Barrett Studio Architects** creates healthy homes that respond to many needs on many levels. Barrett Studio homes are connected to their specific site through climate, responsive and client interactive design solutions, and to the global ecological perspective through sustainable material and energy use. Over twenty-five years of award-winning, full-service design experience leads to spaces that resonate with a timeless beauty and are connected deeply to the roots of our planet — the true embodiment of a living architecture.

1944 20th Street
Boulder, CO 80302
303.449.1141
303.449.9320
bsa@barrettstudio.com

BLBenn Architects, an AIA award-winning firm, has thirty-five years' experience in custom residential and commercial architecture. It strives to create a vital architecture that enhances the human spirit. The firm's practice is committed to the ideal that good design improves the quality of lives and of communities. Its designs emphasize naturally lit interior spaces, simple sculptural volumes, carefully planned layouts, and quality detailing and craftsmanship.

28 1/2 Rip Rd .
Hanover, NH 03755
603.643.5058
BLBenn@valley.net
www.blbennarchitects.com

Peter Brock, Architect is a group of architects and craftspeople in Berkeley, California. For over twenty years, the firm has been making buildings, furniture, and objects of art to meet the needs of diverse clients across a wide spectrum of project scale, geographic setting, and stylistic context. It thrives on close collaborations with owners and artisans engaged in solving unique design challenges with craftsmanship and creative and responsible use of natural materials.

812 Camelia St.,
Berkeley, CA 94710
510.524.2644
www.peter-brock.com

Established in 1975, **Jeremiah Eck Architects** believes that architecture is an art and a service and, most importantly, that good clients make good architecture. Eck is a Fellow of the AIA, author of The *Distinctive Home: A Vision of Timeless Design*, and a landscape painter. His new book, *The Face of Home,* will be published in the spring of 2006. A former lecturer at Harvard University's Graduate School of Design, he continues to offer Professional Development Seminars on Houses; has been featured in numerous architectural books and magazines; and won numerous awards.

560 Harrison Ave.
Suite 403
Boston, MA 02118
617.367.9696
info@jearch.com
www.jearch.com

Established in 1983, **Debra Kay George Interiors** offers a complete design service from consulting and space planning, to selecting, specifying and supplying all the furnishings and materials. With her design and construction knowledge, space-planning talent, and eye for color, Debra coordinates the plan from the beginning architectural phase through to the detailed finishing and furnishing phase. She creates a stunning personalized environment that represents her client's individual taste. Throughout the years, she has participated in many showcase homes and has been featured in publications such as *Silicon Valley Home, Gentry Magazine, California Home and Design,* and the *SJ Mercury News*.

6584 Camden Ave.
San Jose, CA 95120
408.997.1143
debrakg@pacbell.net
debrakaygeorgeinteriors.com

R.S. Granoff Architects p.c. is a full-service architecture, planning and interior design firm dedicated to providing outstanding client service and achieving excellence in architecture. With offices in Greenwich, Connecticut, and Southampton, New York, the firm works on a wide variety of residential and commercial projects throughout the New York metropolitan area. Its philosophy of architecture is balanced between respect for the past and excitement about the future, which has resulted in work of great variety, vitality, and enduring quality.

30 West Putnam Ave.
Greenwich, CT 06830
203.625.9460
rg@granoffarchitects.com
www.granoffarchitects.com

Graymatter Architecture is an energetic, design-oriented architecture studio dedicated to the play of principles relating to space, light, color, materials, and details. Located in Santa Monica, California, it explores new and creative uses of a varied palette of materials and searches for innovative ways of detailing the making of buildings.

639 East Channel Rd.
Santa Monica, CA 90402
310.454.7960
mgray@graymatterarchitecture.com
www.graymatterarchitecture.com

Architectural Digest calls **Jonathan Isleib** of **JBI Design** an "over-achiever in one of New England's most unassuming places," a designer whose work "demonstrates what can be gained by not letting architecture dominate nature." With a repertoire that includes both innovative new construction and meticulous restorations, Isleib is perhaps best known for designs that bear a symbiotic relationship with nature. A collaborative group, JBI Design provides expertise in all aspects of design, from landscape to architecture, space planning to furniture. Isleib's projects have been featured in *Architectural Digest, Interior Design, Christie's Great Estates, Kitchens/Baths, Colonial Homes, Decorating Ideas,* and *House & Garden.*

268 Joshuatown Rd.
Lyme, CT 06371
860.526.5577
jonathan@jbidesign.com

Brion Jeannette & Associates, Inc. began in 1974 with a vision and architectural philosophy that continues to bring notoriety and success to the firm. Its "goal is to design unique and exciting projects that meet our clients' needs and desires and respect their environment. We reach to achieve designs that provide depth and maximize the potential of the site. These goals allow our firm to be as selective about the projects we take, as the clients that seek us." Many of their projects have been precedent setting, requiring strategic planning and cautious negotiation to open the doors for project approvals with homeowner associations, cities, and the California Coastal Commission.

470 Old Newport Blvd.
Newport Beach, CA 92663
949.645.5854
email@customarchitecture.com
www.customarchitecture.com

Maurice Jennings + David McKee Architects provide a full range of architectural services consisting of design, design development, and service during construction. The firm's philosophy in architectural design is rooted in the principles of organic architecture as espoused by Frank Lloyd Wright and their mentor E. Fay Jones. It emphasizes craft and careful attention to detail in the development of projects in all stages. On-site involvement is also a major part of the process, as the firm believes that the architect must have a hands-on role in the implementation of the design.

619 W. Dickson St.
Fayetteville, AR 72701
479.443.4742
jenningsmckee@arkansas.net
www.jenningsmckeearch.com

Joel Karr, an award-winning architect, has practiced architecture in seven countries and on three continents. Having practiced architecture for twenty years in large, internationally recognized commercial architecture firms, he now maintains a small office engaged in residential and small commercial work. His versatility in project work is rooted in his strong belief that collaboration and listening are critical keys to successful project management. His work reflects the care he takes in producing designs of quality, and nurturing great relationships. Joel is also the owner of Group 41 Incorporated, a small residential developer in the San Francisco Bay Area.

41 Seward St.
San Francisco, CA 94114
415.572.5033
www.group41inc.com

Ming Lee, Architect, established his office in 2001. He currently practices in the greater bay area of Northern California and has had experience with clients abroad, including China, Malaysia, Trinidad, and Germany. Lee is a past president of American Society of Engineers and Architects, obtained his Bachelors of Architecture from California Polytechnic of San Luis Obispo, and attended a one-year study in Florence, Italy. There he became one of only sixty students out of hundreds to be accepted to the Accademia di Belle Arti in Florence.

725 Buchanan St.
Albany CA 94706

510.528.8370
mlee@mingleearch.com
www.mingleearch.com

Donald C. Mallow, Architect, specializes in residential architecture in which the needs of the site and the owner's program are integrated within the expressive nature of space, the selection of materials, and careful detailing, including the design of landscaping and furniture and rugs related to the building design. *The Architectural Record* has referred to his work as "timeless modern architecture."

103 Glenwood Ave.
Leonia, NJ 07605
201.947.1510

94 Salt Pond Road
Blue Hill, ME, 04614
207.374.2111
www.donaldmallow.com

Moiseev/Gordon Associates, Inc. (MGA) is a full service architectural and interior design firm providing services that meet the functional and aesthetic demands of today's buildings. MGA emphasizes service and concentrates on quality within the design process, working in close collaboration with vendors and subcontractors to facilitate a successful design solution. It takes an active role in all aspects of the project, stressing attention to detail, active client involvement, and sensitivity to budget and schedules.

818 W. 11 Mile Rd.
Royal Oak, MI 48067
248.541.2388
Kimberly@moiseev-gordon.com
www.moiseev-gordon.com

Since the founding of **Moore Ruble Yudell** in 1977, the principals have built a varied body of work ranging from private residences to multimillion-dollar institutional, civic, and mixed-use developments. Their work on a wide range of building types has given them extensive experience working with complex client groups as well as regulatory and governmental agencies. The firm has received numerous major awards for design excellence. In 1992 the California Council of the AIA honored it as Firm of the Year.

933 Pico Blvd.
Santa Monica, CA 90405
310.450.1400
info@mryarchitects.com
www.moorerubleyudell.com

Robert Harvey Oshatz, Architect, states that his relationship with his clients is based on a mutual understanding that architecture is the synthesis of logic and emotion. "The architect is the client's artist, creator, logician of an evolving aesthetic structure; a designer of not only the visual but also internal space. My commitment is to interrupt the individual poetic sense of each building site with my client's functional, emotional and spiritual needs. The challenge is to translate that spirit into architectural poetry. When an emotional idea is taken to its logical conclusion, a structure reflecting the client's dream and fantasies is brought into reality."

PO Box 19091
Portland, OR 97219
503.635.4243
robert@oshatz.com
www.oshatz.com

Prairie Wind Architecture p.c., has undertaken a variety of projects ranging from room remodeling to a fifty-unit housing development. The firm's cost estimates are highly accurate in an area where remoteness, the hidden nature of the work, and the idiosyncratic character of the buildings make estimating difficult. Licensed in Wyoming and Montana, Jeff Shelden, principal, provides his clients with "authentic'" Montana architecture and design because of his background in historic preservation, and his work in the Glacier National Park area. "I like living and working here—I want my buildings to speak to that, rather than to say something about me," he says.

Box 626
Lewistown, MT 59457
406.538.2201
pwa@midrivers.com

RKD Architects, Inc. is an award-winning firm specializing in resort and mountain architecture. With offices in Vail, Colorado, and San Francisco, California, RKD has designed and built many residences as well as commercial projects throughout Vail Valley, Lake Tahoe, San Francisco, California, Idaho, Utah, Florida, and New Jersey. Currently, the firm has a number of custom residences on the boards, including several smaller scale, environmentally sensitive homes and three larger scale homes in Telluride, Cordillera, and Mountain Star.

P.O. Box 5055
Edwards, CO 81632

Riverwalk – Diamond Building
137 Main St., Suite G004
Edwards, CO 81632
970.926.2622
rkd@rkdarch.com
www.rkdarch.com

After over twenty-five years working in architecture and design contributing to project types including offices, stores, restaurants, museums, laboratories, mixed use, and residential all over the world, Kathryn Shaffer began **Kathy Shaffer Architecture & Design** in 2004 with the intent of focusing her design expertise on residential projects. Her work emphasizes the use of light and color and draws upon native materials and historical typology.

Her small firm operates out of Sausalito, California, and covers the entire San Francisco Bay Area.

117 Crescent Ave.
Sausalito, CA 94965
415.332.8430
ks@kathyshafferarchitect.com
www.kathyshafferarchitect.com

Stelle Architects is an award-winning architecture, planning, and interior design firm that specializes in the design of educational, cultural, and institutional buildings, as well as coastal residences. Founded in 1984, Stelle Architects is equally adept in the design of new buildings, adaptive reuse, and expansion of historic structures. With every project, the firm strives to produce architecture of formal and functional simplicity, aesthetic integrity, and vision. Every project is a new beginning, and no two are alike.

48 Foster Ave.
P.O. Box 3002
Bridgehampton, NY 11932
631.537.0019
info@stelleco.com
www.stelleco.com

Stevens Architect, LLC, located in Bend, Oregon, is a boutique architectural and urban design firm, where the principal is involved from inception to conception to completion. Throughout his forty-year career, Don Stevens, AIA, has applied his experience and design skills for community centers, award-winning senior centers, and custom residences. The firm is renown for its custom work, attention to detail, and its high standards in designing and developing beautiful, unique, and efficient homes.

1133 NW Wall St., Ste. 200
Bend, OR 97701
541.317.8880

Celebrating over 37 years of service as a successful, multi-disciplinary design firm, **Trout Architects** is committed to the built environment with a philosophy of openness and interaction. It fully engages clients in the design process by encompassing their values and vision. The firm's solutions are a synthesis of this input, producing the highest level of design. The firm believes that designers today must be environmentally aware and conscious of bettering a quality of life as they build a new living or work environment.

1030 La Pointe
Boise, ID 83706
208.344.8646
troutarchitects.com
www.troutarchitects.com

Joseph Henry Wythe studied under his mentor, Bruce Goff at the University of Oklahoma. For several years following graduation in 1948, Wythe remained at University of Oklahoma to teach design and several technical courses. Returning to California, Wythe opened his studio in Monterey. At the local community college, he taught an innovative beginning course in architecture, which became so successful that students transferring to the University reported receiving two years of credit for the one-year course at Monterey. In 1977, Wythe moved to Sandpoint, Idaho, where he established his studio under the name of Alternative Architecture and later constructed his home and studio.

wythe@sandpoint.net

James E. Zervas, who studied under Frank Lloyd Wright during an apprenticeship at Taliesin, founded **Zervas Group Architects** in 1961. Accolades for the firm's exceptional work have included numerous awards from the Northwest Washington Chapter of the American Institute of Architects, the City of Bellingham, the Washington Masonry Asso-

ciation, the National Association of Housing and Redevelopment Officials, and a Grand Award from the Custom Home Design Awards, sponsored by *Custom Home* and *Residential Architecture* magazines.

209 Prospect St.
Bellingham, WA 98225
360.734.4744
info@zervasgroup.com
www.zervasgroup.com

Other Resources

American Ingenuity manufactures the dome shell kit, which is shipped to the construction site. It has dome houses in forty-seven states and seven foreign areas. A super strong, energy-efficient, low maintenance dome home can be finished turn key for about the same price per square foot as a conventional house.

8777 Holiday Springs Rd.
Rockledge, Fl 32955
321.639.8777
info@aidomes.com
www.aidomes.com

Entrusted to Western Pennsylvania Conservancy, **Fallingwater** has been acclaimed "the best all-time work of American architecture" and one of the "Top 50 Places of a Lifetime. It is open mid-March through November for tours. Reservations are essential. For more information, call 724.329.8501 or visit www.paconserve.org.

PT BPT BaliClavis developed an innovative model "kit house" called the "TomaHouseBaleClassic." Its lightweight aluminum structures, designed and fabricated in Germany, are transportable anywhere, making it ideal for more moderate and warmer climates. Utilizing natural elements such as wood, stones, and natural fibers, it combines German technology with the charm of Balinese craftsmanship.

TomaHouse
Bali Indonesia
+62 361.7432723
pt@tomahouse.com
www.tomahouse.com

Timberpeg® has been designing and fabricating timber frame homes and commercial structures for over thirty years. With representatives around the nation and around the world, Timberpeg® works with its clients providing service throughout the entire process to ensure building a timber frame is an enjoyable experience.

info@timberpeg.com
www.timberpeg.com

Todos Santos Eco Adventures (TOSEA) helps visitors explore the natural, cultural, and culinary delights of an unspoiled Mexican town located in Baja. TOSEA's vacation packages feature incredible encounters with the local flora and fauna through spectacular cliff walks, swims with sea lion puppies, treks to desert waterfalls, trips to release newborn turtles into the sea, and walks in the protected Biosphere Reserve.

TOSEA introduces guests to some of the several artists living in town, as well as many of the terrific restaurants that draw visitors from all over Baja.

011-5. 612.145.0780
info@tosea.net
www.tosea.net

Winterwood Lakeside Cottage is an Adirondack-styled "get away" tucked into the woods along the secluded shores of Beaver Lake. Here, with more than eighty acres of private woods at your door step, a visitor can hike, swim, picnic or simply sit on the verandah and enjoy the breathtaking view of the lake, a private dock, and the surrounding mountains. Crafted of oak and Douglas fir, the cottage is a throw back to a time when building was an art, and rustic luxury was a way of life. Owned by Winterwood Recording Studios, it has been visited by the stars since 1996. Today, the cottage is now being offered to individuals outside of the industry as well. Its staff has earned over 100 gold and multi platinum albums worldwide.

Eureka Springs, Arkansas 72632
479.253.2530
Winterwdcottage@aol.com
www.winterwoodstudios.com
www.winterwoodlakesidecottage.com

Index